Kim —
Thanks for
coming. Enjoy the
Book. Pick
Prepa
tions
Happy
Cooking
Cocktails
+
Entertaining
XO
Sandra

FLOWERS

LULUPOWERS
FOODTOFLOWERS

SIMPLE, STYLISH FOOD FOR EASY ENTERTAINING

WITH LAURA HOLMES HADDAD
PHOTOGRAPHS BY STEPHEN DANELIAN

wm WILLIAM MORROW *An Imprint of* HarperCollins*Publishers*

HarperCollins books may be purchased for educational, business, or sales promotional use. For information please write: Special Markets Department, HarperCollins Publishers, 10 East 53rd Street, New York, NY 10022.

FIRST EDITION

Designed by *Air-Conditioned*

Library of Congress Cataloging-in-Publication Data

Powers, Lulu.
  Lulu Powers food to flowers: simple, stylish food for easy entertaining / Lulu Powers with Laura Holmes Haddad; with photographs by Stephen Danelian.—1st ed.
     p.   cm.
  Includes index.
  ISBN 978-0-06-149327-0
  1. Entertaining. 2. Cookery. I. Haddad, Laura Holmes. II. Title.
TX731.P688 2009
793.2—dc22
                         2008037696

10 11 12 13 14 ov/LEO 10 9 8 7 6 5 4 3 2 1

To my husband, Stephen Danelian, a.k.a. Stevie D, my rock. You make me a better person every day . . . thank you!

And to my mom, Patti P.; my sisters, Sue, Julie, Sarah, and Molly; and my dear brother, Byrne. Thanks for always being there for me . . . you make me tick!

In honor of my father, James Beston Powers, my best friend, who always loved and inspired me. "It's puurrfectttt!" *Toy always.* Go Sox!

To my "Auntie Mame," Patti Altman, who taught me that entertaining is fun and that it's okay to have ice cream for breakfast.

To my dear friend Andrea Coscia, who always said, "You can do anything, LB." Your quick wit is sorely missed.

To Alma: Well, you're in the book. You're unforgettable. I miss you, buddy!

CONTENTS

At Pike's Market in Seattle, home of wonderful food and flowers

INTRODUCTION

I grew up in a boisterous family of six kids in Connecticut. My first memory of entertaining is of refilling drinks from the bar and serving mushroom croustades at my parents' parties, where my four sisters and brother and I would all make an appearance. Even at eight years old, I knew the party was a success when people were laughing and having fun—and they'd still be talking and laughing at 1:00 A.M., when I put myself to bed. My parents loved to entertain, and our house was like Grand Central Station with people stopping by all the time to eat and visit. So it wasn't a surprise that after cooking for endless cocktail and dinner soirées—not to mention all those kids—my mom opened her own catering business. With no formal training, my mom planned parties for anywhere from twenty to six hundred people without batting an eye.

My mom hired my sisters, our friends, and me. I loved being an integral part of the homespun kitchen crew, otherwise known as the Patti Powers Country Cuisine staff.

At fifteen, having worked for my mom for several years, I lied about my age and got a job as a counter girl for Sarah Leah Chase, a famous Nantucket gourmand who owned a gourmet food shop called Que Sera Sarah. I soon realized after my first summer there that I was more knowledgeable about food than I thought. My customers listened intently as I suggested creative food pairings and how to prepare simple yet amazing desserts.

Fast forward a few years. I was holding cooking classes in my urban New York City apartment and was eager to share my expertise with others. But my true culinary adventure began when I moved to Los Angeles to become a television writer. After helping a friend with her child's birthday, three mothers asked me to cater their kids' parties and Lulu Powers Food to Flowers was born. One celebrity gig led to another and before long I was a private chef to a cache of major Hollywood stars.

Eventually I started teaching casual cooking classes, this time in a more expansive kitchen in L.A., instructing my students in the art of cooking as well as entertaining. I gave them ideas for delicious and beautiful party food and taught them how to throw a successful cocktail party for thirty.

I've thrown thousands of soirées since helping my mother grow her business, from intimate dinners for two to colossal fifteen-hundred-person fetes. (An education that really began when I learned that a drink should always be served with a cocktail napkin.) Now I want to share the entertaining acumen I've accumulated over the years with you.

Entertaining can be a scary word. Hosts and hostesses often start out excited, filled with good intentions, but quickly become overwhelmed and anxious when, as the party nears, they haven't yet decided what to cook or how to serve it.

I've walked friends and clients through what I call "Party Phobia," and so far everyone's come through with flying colors. Even if it seems that everything is going wrong, the worst thing that could happen is that you have to order pizza. Fear is like fire: you can either cook with it or let it burn you—literally! One night I was invited to dinner at a friend's house. We were at the table when I smelled something burning. It turned out that the apple tarts had burned and dessert was ruined. But like an actor who needs to improvise after forgetting his lines, so must the cook. I ushered my distressed friend to the kitchen and we effortlessly whipped up another dessert. With vanilla ice cream, peanut butter, and chocolate chips at hand, I showed my wide-eyed friend how to make a two-minute peanut butter sauce. We topped the ice cream with the quick confection, sprinkled on some chocolate chips, and dessert was saved.

When using this book, remember that you can use any of these recipes for any of the parties. Just pick and choose. You're the chef—be creative!

My philosophy is that you should adapt recipes to your taste; you shouldn't have to replicate them exactly. Make these recipes and ideas your own and come up with your own signature dish or party. And most important, trust your instincts!

It's always better to have more food than less; I don't mind having leftovers. After you throw a few parties, you'll get a feel for how much food you need and what your friends like.

I live by my favorite saying from Auntie Mame: "Live, live, live. Life's a banquet and most poor suckers are starving to death."

PARTIES Rx

Here are a bunch of tips and shortcuts to take the stress out of entertaining and help you throw a flawless party. I've collected these tips throughout my years in business, from my first job working for my mom, a caterer, up through the thousands of parties I've thrown or planned for friends and clients. I've seen it all, and trust me: once you know these tips you can throw a great party too.

THE BEST-KEPT SECRET: PARTY RENTALS

Rentals take the stress out of any party, and these days you can rent everything from glasses, plates, serving platters, and silverware to doughnut makers, coffee machines, and In-N-Out Burger trucks (an incredible family-owned hamburger chain based in Los Angeles with outrageously delicious hamburgers and fries); even Carl's Jr. rents mobile catering trucks. But check your local area for rental ideas. In Nantucket you can rent an ice cream truck, and in Connecticut I discovered a great pizza truck that will cater any event. Find a fun rental and plan your party around that.

If you have enough room to store an extra fifty wine and/or Champagne glasses, great. If not, rent. If you do have storage space, you can always buy good, inexpensive glasses at stores like Cost Plus World Market, Target, and many others. And if your budget allows, renting dishes, silverware, and glassware makes throwing a party even easier—most companies drop off and pick everything up, and you don't have to wash a thing or worry about breaking one of your own glasses or plates.

Adding something unexpected to a party is always a great idea, and fun things like photo booths, cotton candy machines, and chocolate fountains are a few ways to add a twist to the event. I've rented photo booths for holiday parties and weddings, and they're a huge hit. Who doesn't love to pose—and then have the instant gratification of that little photo strip? And chocolate fountains turn adults into little kids and put a smile on everyone's face.

You'd be surprised at what's available for rent, including candleholders and hurricane lamps. I've rented couches, coffee tables, chandeliers, mirrors—almost anything you can think of, down to a great old wooden bar. Beyond regular party rental stores, you can also rent virtually anything from prop houses, and if you don't have a prop house near you, most home stores will rent furniture and home accessories for a percentage of the retail price.

HIRING HELP

Hiring bartenders and wait staff can ease the party jitters. The rates for staffing vary depending on your location and the company you use. Staffing services are usually a little more expensive than staff you hire yourself. If you need help at a party, ask a waiter or bartender from a local restaurant that you frequent or get a recommendation from a friend. Friends' kids can sometimes help out, even if it's just busing dishes and cleaning the kitchen. If you live near a college or culinary school, contact the career office and hire students as wait staff and bartenders. And depending on where you live, a valet parking service can be helpful. If you do use a valet service and it's a big party, it's nice to have beverages, such as bottled water, hot chocolate, or coffee, available near the valet stand for guests to drink while they wait for their cars.

I always ask my servers to wear a uniform, because it looks clean and sleek. The clothes depend on the party; for a kids' party I ask my staff to wear jeans, a belt, and a white button-down shirt, while for an evening soirée I ask them to dress in all black with a tie. (I find that all black looks more chic than black pants and a white shirt.) Depending on the party, I might also have them wear bistro aprons, half-aprons that come in white and black, available at most kitchen stores (I always have extras on hand in case the staff has forgotten them). My clients often come up with their own uniforms for the staff. For a holiday party one client bought my staff Santa Claus aprons, which they wore over white shirts and black pants. A client who was throwing a magazine launch party bought lime green Lacoste shirts for my staff and asked them to wear white pants. For a wedding I threw, the client asked the staff to wear pink button-down shirts and supplied them with Lilly Pulitzer ties.

If you've hired someone to help you (bartender, waiter, or kitchen help), it's a good idea to hold an informal staff meeting before the party.

Start the meeting by thanking them and then set out their responsibilities: Servers should make sure no dirty glasses are lying around and ashtrays are emptied, and if the buffet looks messy, they should take it upon themselves to tidy it up. Let them run the show; give them the power. (They will do a better job if they feel they have some sort of ownership.) If you're serving passed appetizers, they should circulate new platters of food in a timely manner.

Designate one person to check the bathroom occasionally to make sure it's clean. If it looks as if you're running out of booze or ice, the bartenders shouldn't wait until they're on the last bottle before telling you; they need to give you a chance to call and order more liquor or hit the reserve stashes. Ice is cheap, so buy extra. The last thing you want to be doing is running to the store for more ice! If you don't have room in your freezer, keep bags of ice in the washing machine; any melted ice will drain right out. You can also buy hot-cold food bags and throw your frozen stuff into the bags while storing the ice in the freezer; your frozen items will stay frozen in the bags for at least eight hours.

If the waiter, bartender, and kitchen staff did a great job, tips are in order. At my own parties I pay 20 percent in gratuity, as you would in a restaurant. (I waitressed, and I know how much work it is.) Of course, my clients' tipping rates vary: at a recent party my staff each received a $40 tip, while at another event the client gave everyone a $100 tip plus hourly wages.

PARTY 911: SOLUTIONS FOR PARTY EMERGENCIES

Stain Removal: Inevitably, if you're having a party, things will spill. You just have to be prepared. The most obvious stain is red wine on white carpet, white clothing, or light-colored furniture. To remove the stain, make a paste with OxiClean and use a toothbrush to scrub it on the stain. Let it sit, rinse it off, and repeat. Another favorite is the Tide Stick, which is an easy way to remove stains from both clothing and furniture. There's also a solution called Wine Away that will do in a pinch (see Sources). The Mr. Clean Magic Eraser is another lifesaver; it cleans furniture and even walls. My latest obsession is Dawn dishwashing liquid, which I use on my walls to remove dirt, scrapes, and stains as well as clothing stains. (It even removes fleas, a tip I got from my dog groomer, Tony!) If there's wax stuck to glass or silver candlesticks, put them in the freezer for an hour or two and the wax will come right off. To remove wax from a table, cover the wax with a paper towel and then lay a dishcloth on top. Using a warm iron, iron the dishcloth. The wax will adhere to the paper towel and peel right off. The same process can be used to remove wax from a coat or tablecloth.

When Your Friends Bring (Uninvited) Friends: Don't make them feel bad—just go with it and don't panic! Keep smiling and see my advice on stocking a Party Pantry (page 22). If your cupboards are bare, food is just a phone call away: you can always call for pizza, cut it up, and serve it on a cutting board to stretch the food you're already serving. Keep a stack of take-out menus from nearby restaurants in a drawer and pull out paper plates if you don't have enough dishes. People don't mind a bare-bones dinner as long as everyone is having a good time—they're just glad they didn't have to make it themselves. Even if you're serving takeout, light candles, put the music on, and have fun!

Emergency Snacks: I keep a stack of six bowls in my pantry for last-minute guests, and I fill them with snacks like potato chips, Goldfish crackers, dried apricots, wasabi peas, snow pea crisps, and banana chips. Any set of bowls will do, as long as they match. Even Bambu disposable bowls will work (see Sources). One set of six serving bowls is ideal—just invest in a set of matching bowls and your entertaining will look effortless. When you repeat the same design element, it keeps the look together and makes you seem prepared. If six is too many for you in terms of storage, buy in threes: three vases, bowls, or plates look great. And you can always use a round or square widemouthed vase as a bowl to put your treats in.

Lulu's Tip

When you're serving small snacks such as nuts or wasabi peas, use a 2-cup bowl. It's the perfect size because it's not so small that you have to keep refilling it.

When Mother Nature Doesn't Cooperate: The weather can wreak havoc with even the best party plans. Check the forecast three days ahead and make a plan if it isn't what you desire it to be. If rain or snow is predicted, place some old towels by the door so that guests can wipe their feet. Set up something outside the front door for umbrellas so they don't drip everywhere (or stick them in the bathtub or shower). Clear out your coat closet, spread garbage bags on the floor, and hang up guests' wet coats. If it starts to rain during the party, hand out garbage bags as makeshift raincoats and Ziploc bags to cover your guests' heads. An inexpensive clothes rack from a store such as Target or Bed Bath & Beyond is an easy solution if you don't have a coat closet or don't want guests piling wet coats in the bedroom.

For an outdoor party, don't schedule a rain date—bring it inside instead. If you've reserved an outdoor space at a restaurant, like a patio, make sure it can be covered. And remember, there's always a rental tent available. When it started raining before one of my own parties, I quickly threw up a portable frame tent with a vinyl top I had found at Kmart and set up the bar outside my covered front door. A tent may not be the prettiest structure, but adding your own touches can really jazz it up, whether it's balloons, swaths of fabric, holiday lights, or large branches. And you can customize a tent: take the vinyl top to a seamstress and have her replace it with your favorite fabric. (Look for discount outdoor fabric, such as Sunbrella brand fabric, online.) Whether or not it's raining, it's fun to set up the bar outside. For an outdoor bar, I like to place a lamp or two on the bar, or some candles, to make it look homey.

MY HOSTESS TRICKS

As the daughter of a caterer, I've found that party planning and entertaining have always come naturally to me. But what I've learned is that even if you're not a planner, if you take a few minutes to write out a menu, find recipes, or make lists of groceries or entertaining supplies such as candles, you can minimize your stress level. Don't be afraid to jump in, and what initially seems scary will begin to seem quite manageable. Remember that the key to any party, big or small, is the host or hostess. *You* set the mood of the party.

Make Your House Welcoming: There's nothing more inviting than walking into a house and smelling something lovely. Some people don't like strong scents, but I'm crazy about them: flowers, candles, incense, pine, cinnamon, coffee—you name it.

My favorite trick is to buy refrigerated cookie dough and bake the cookies as the guests arrive. (Or make my own cookie dough, freeze it, and bake it as needed.) Arrange the cookies on a cake plate and set them on a countertop— you can even put them in a fun jar or short round vase. Just be creative!

To create an inviting scent, you can also boil apple cider on the stove with a handful of cloves or cinnamon sticks; the scent is divine. An easy shortcut is to brew apple-cinnamon or

orange spice tea bags. My mom loves to heat up a saucepan of fresh cider mixed with cranberry juice and cinnamon sticks, which smells heavenly and makes a great party drink.

Nail Down the Timing: This takes practice, and after a few parties you'll have it mastered. Here are guidelines to get you started for both planned and impromptu events.

* **Two Weeks Ahead:** For a big party, plan your menu and make sure your pantry items are stocked. When planning your menu, think seasonally and remember that you can cook and decorate with seasonal ingredients. If you have children, make sure to book a babysitter for the duration of the party. You don't want to be running after the kids or putting them to bed while entertaining a houseful of guests. (One of my clients solved this problem by sending the babysitter and the kids to a hotel for the night!)

* **The Day Before:** Whether the party is big or small, shop and start to prep one day ahead of time. Buy all the ingredients and make what you can at least one day before the party. Planning to serve a salsa, a peppercorn sauce, cookies, or a chocolate cake? Make it ahead of time. Once you start to check things off your checklist, your shoulders will drop and you'll feel less stressed. Buy items such as flowers and herbs the day before or cut branches or flowers from your garden.

* **The Night Before:** Pick out what you're going to wear to the party and try it on to avert any last-minute clothing crises. (If it's a casual dinner with friends, don't worry about this.)

* **That Morning:** Go over your party list and double-check that you have everything you need; run out to the store for any last-minute items. Make your to-do list on sticky notes—one item per note—and pull them off as you finish each task.

* **One Hour Before:** Make sure your kitchen is clean—the floor swept; the dishes washed, dried,

> **LULU'S TIP FOR GUESTS**
> I wouldn't dream of showing up at someone's house for a party empty-handed. A hostess gift shows that you appreciate being invited, and it can just be something small like an elegant candle, your favorite chocolates, or your kid's homemade cookies. Choose something you love, whether it's a bottled steak sauce or a jar of jam. It's a small gesture that speaks volumes.

and put away; and your dishwasher empty. Be sure the countertop is wiped down with a fresh-smelling spray (there are wonderful kitchen sprays scented with parsley or citrus; see Sources).

Put napkins out and light the candles. Make sure the ice is out and the wine is chilled. (If you've forgotten to chill the wine, you can chill it in twenty minutes by putting it in a bucket filled with half ice half water and a handful of kosher salt.) If you're throwing a dinner party, have tea out and fill the coffeepot or press with ground coffee. (Even at a cocktail party, people ask for coffee, so be prepared.) Make sure you have herbal tea or decaffeinated coffee available as well and have sugar and/or Splenda and milk or cream ready. (Although I prefer natural sugar, many people use artificial sweeteners.) Turn on your outdoor lights, if necessary. Put the music on.

✳ **Thirty Minutes Before:** Get dressed a half hour before the party starts; you never know who will come early. If you have extra time, close your eyes for a ten-minute power nap. Take a moment to pour yourself a drink and relax.

✳ **Ten Minutes Before:** Someone needs to greet your guests at the door, whether it's the host, an appointed friend, or a helper. Greet the guests with a hello, *bonjour,* or greeting in any language—just make them feel welcome. If you can, leave the front door unlocked so people can let themselves in and you don't have to run to the door every minute. Regardless, the host or an appointed greeter should always meet guests as they arrive.

The most important thing to remember as a host or hostess is always to offer your guests a beverage upon entry. There is nothing worse than trying to find the host and standing around without a beverage. People feel more comfortable when they have something to hold, especially when they don't know anyone.

✳ **During the Party:** Check the food and the bar and replenish as necessary (or ask a friend to keep an eye on the buffet, clear any dirty glasses, and let you know if the bathroom looks messy). About three-quarters of the way through a cocktail party, I like to put out some sweets in addition to the candy I already have out. Don't make your guests the kitchen audience or the kitchen staff unless you've invited them over specifically to cook dinner together. Having your guests watch you prepare dinner is a yawn. My husband and I went to a dinner party that was enjoyable except for the fact that the chef, also known as the host, was in the kitchen the whole time.

> **LULU'S TIP FOR GUESTS**
> If you're shy, just smile and be friendly, and someone is bound to say hello and talk to you. If I'm at a party where I don't know a soul, I strike up a conversation with a bartender. Inevitably someone else comes up to the bar, and I end up meeting someone new.

✳ **After the Party:** After you've eaten, clear the table and put the dirty dishes in the sink. Remove just the plates and any serving dishes; if you remove everything from the table, guests will think the party is over. Get a plastic tub, throw the dishes in, and clean up *after* your guests leave. (I even had to teach my own husband to leave the dishes until later.) When the dishes are cleared, put out a little bowl of sweets like cookies, malt balls, or truffles on the table while you're making the coffee or bringing the dessert out. After a very garlicky meal, I always pass around a pretty bowl filled with miniature boxes of Chiclets. I like to make coffee and tea in a French press, but if you want to prepare them in advance, serve them in carafes (see Sources). It's not a must-do, but it will simplify things if you're easily overwhelmed. Make sure to warm the milk too. It's up to you to decide which direction the dinner party—or any party—will take at that point. You can put on some upbeat music and serve after-dinner drinks to keep the party going or turn the music down and let people start to say their good-byes.

THE GOOD HOST

Whether it's cocktails for a hundred or drinks for two good friends, being a good host is key; host etiquette applies to every event. If people don't know each other, introduce them. I threw one party where I had invited so many people who didn't know each other that I put signs around the party on menu boards that said, "If you don't know someone, introduce yourself." If you think it's appropriate, you could also make fun name tags to help guests remember people's names. Another conversation starter

Sample Party Time Line

Party: a ten-person dinner party

Menu: cheese and crackers, nuts, and figs with goat cheese and prosciutto; marinated grilled steak; grilled shrimp; salad; and dessert

The Night Before: Set the table and stick beer and wine in the fridge. Don't wait to marinate the steak the day of the party—prep ahead of time. Other basic tasks like deveining shrimp should be done the night before. (And if you're serving a sauce with the steak, make it the day ahead.) Also, wash the greens and store them in paper towels in the refrigerator. Make the salad dressing.

That Night: Bring the steaks to room temperature and prepare them for the grill. If you know your side dish will take forty minutes, stick it in the oven either before your guests arrive or forty minutes before you plan to serve dinner. You can either leave it in the oven on low to stay warm or take it out and stick it back in the oven about fifteen minutes before you sit down to eat.

that's great for a dinner party is TableTopics, small preprinted cards with conversation-starting topics that you can put at each place setting (see Sources). I make a party fun; that is the key. With a fun host, great food, and good music, people want to stay and hang out.

Last, but certainly not least, if you're nervous, anxious, or irritated before or even during the party, go into the pantry and scream—but don't take it out on your guests. If you've had a disagreement with your husband, partner, sibling, or friend, take a deep breath and put a smile on your face. Don't make your guests want to leave just because you're upset.

LIGHTING

The last trick: use candlelight whenever possible. I love any kind of candle—whatever you have, use it. Just make sure you have the right size candles for your candleholders. If you don't have candleholders, use vases or ashtrays; even juice glasses will work for tea light candles. A silver bowl filled with tea lights creates ambience. And you can always stick a candle in the first empty wine bottle. I have a client whose friend always asks me, "Why does the house look better every time you're here?" My response is "I lowered the lights and lit some candles." Candles give any room a warm, cozy feeling.

Don't burn scented candles where you'll be eating; they'll interfere with the flavors of the food. However, they can be useful while you're cooking. Since I'm obsessed with candles, I keep a citrus-cilantro candle in my kitchen, and when I cook fish—or occasionally burn something—it really helps absorb the odors. (Yes, I do burn things, and that's why I attach a timer to my apron.) Or leave a bowl of coffee grounds on the counter to absorb any lingering odors. There are great kitchen sprays you can use to get rid of cooking odors (see Sources for candles and cooking sprays).

For a poolside or outdoor party, fill stemless plastic wineglasses with dried beans and place votive candles in them. You can use any kind of bean, pink lentils, rice, salt, or even little pebbles, which you can find at a garden store. The bottom line is that everyone looks better in low light!

INVITATIONS

I like getting pretty invitations in the mail—who doesn't? But while beautiful stationery is an affordable luxury, there isn't always time to get a nice invite ready for a party. For a last-minute gathering, I prefer to call people on the phone, but cocodot.com and paperlesspost.com offer great, convenient ways to send invitations and thank-you notes too. For more special gatherings, of course, nothing beats a really cool invitation you receive through the mail.

When you create invitations—paper or electronic—don't forget to give directions to your place or the party location so guests can use a Web site to get directions (and be sure to include the zip code). I expect people to RSVP, and I always give them the option to call or email. Just remember that in these busy times not everyone will respond; for a party with sixty invited guests, count on thirty RSVPs, while probably forty-five people will show. If you're really concerned about the head count, you could send out a reminder via email, although it's not my preferred method.

Surprise parties are hard to pull off, but if you're throwing one, make sure you send a paper invitation—you never know whom someone will forward an email to. It's also a good idea to put "shhh" in the heading of the invite. You could also easily set up an email account just for the party and have responses sent to that email address.

Etiquette also applies to guests: You should always thank your host after the party. A handwritten thank-you note mailed to your host is always preferable, but if you really don't have time, email or text is better than nothing. Buy pretty stationery to use as thank-you notes or buy a rubber stamp and stamp plain paper to create your own custom stationery (see Sources for stationery and paper ideas).

SETTING THE TABLE

Here are a few easy decorating ideas for table centerpieces:

* Fill a glass vase or wooden bowl with a dozen green or red apples, persimmons, tangerines, lemons, or limes. A vase or basket filled with branches is also striking.

* Plants look great lined up on a table; always work in threes. I like miniature cacti and other succulents and little citrus trees. You can find miniature plants at a garden store, a ninety-nine-cent or dollar store, and many others.

* If you collect something, like pretty bottles, group them together and use what you have to make centerpieces. For example, line a collection of antique lunch boxes down the middle of the table, open them up, and stick some plants in them or fill them with candy.

* Anything can be made into a centerpiece. As a last resort, just arrange tea lights in glass vases on the table; they're inexpensive and easily found at stores like Crate & Barrel and Pottery Barn.

* An unexpected use for a beautiful handbag is to showcase it on the table. Simply find a sturdy, stylish bag, place a bunch of flowers in a small cylindrical vase, and set the vase in the handbag. Use a piece of burlap fabric as the tablecloth. (Ballard's sells great inexpensive lined burlap tablecloths, or visit a fabric store.) I planned a breast cancer benefit where guests purchased pairs of shoes for charity. I created centerpieces out of beautiful shoes, wrapping posies with green ribbon and placing them inside the shoes. To complete the look, find colorful silk scarves at a thrift or vintage store and use them as napkins. The scarves make great gifts for your guests to take home. It's bohemian chic.

* One thing I always do at my parties is put the menu in a picture frame. Just print a menu on the computer and use an old frame or cover up a photo in your favorite frame. I also like to put a drink menu on the bar so people know what's available. If it's a buffet, use small frames to display the names of each dish. Even if you're having two people over for dinner, it's fun to put a little menu on the table.

Instead of frames, you can write directly on porcelain. Anything made of white porcelain can be written on with a Sharpie pen and simply wiped off with a cloth. I have a whole set of porcelain bowls, menu boards, and vases, and I write on them all the time—SALT, SUGAR, the name of a menu item, whatever. It really personalizes the event. If your handwriting isn't great, get a friend with nice penmanship to do it. (If you want to write something permanently, use a paint pen.)

If you don't have a porcelain menu board or a frame, just take a small salad or dessert plate and write the menu or a welcome note on it using a Sharpie pen. Prop the plate up on a plate stand, if you have one, or a display stand, available at art supply stores.

TABLE DÉCOR

✱ Glasses don't have to match. Focus instead on what's inside the glasses: great cocktails or refreshing sippers.

✱ I use plain cotton dish towels as napkins (I got the idea from Balthazar restaurant in New York City), and my husband prefers them to regular napkins. Just keep a separate stash from the ones you use for the kitchen. Buy one type of towel; it just looks more polished if you use matching towels.

✱ I like to keep a selection of tablecloths on hand. You can buy fabric (remnant fabric is a great bargain) at any fabric store (even IKEA has great fabrics), and if you don't sew, take it to a local seamstress or tailor to make a hem. If you have a basic, neutral-colored tablecloth, use a piece of brightly colored fabric as a table runner. If you have only one set of dishes, tablecloths are a great way to expand your table décor options.

✱ I also use brightly colored place mats that are easy to clean and store. Fun place mats make plain white plates pop on the table, and they dress up a plain wood table. An easy, inexpensive way to create a place mat is by using colored construction paper. It comes in millions of colors and sizes and you can write the name of each guest on top of the paper. It's a perfect solution for adults and kids. The right place mat can make even plastic plates look great.

✱ To jazz up a set of white napkins, roll the napkins and tie them with a pretty ribbon. Insert a sprig of fresh rosemary or lavender or a small ribbon. Napkin holders dress up even the most basic outdoor table.

Party Checklist: House

O Is your kitchen clean?

O Is the dishwasher or dish rack empty?

O Bathrooms:

Do all the bathrooms have toilet paper? Fresh hand towels or guest towels? Hand soap and hand cream? Room spray? (My favorite is Cucina brand; see Sources.)

Are the cabinets stocked with extra personal products (tampons, Band-Aids, Chiclets or Altoids, Tylenol or Advil, disposable toothbrushes and toothpaste, dental floss or flavored toothpicks, mouthwash, baby powder, spray deodorant, small nail scissors, and a nail file)? You can buy small sizes in the travel section of the drugstore.

O Is the house too warm or too cool? Open windows, turn up the heat— do whatever you need to do to make the environment comfortable. But remember that a lot of bodies will heat a space up.

O Outdoor patio heaters can heat up an outdoor space quickly and efficiently and keep your guests warm on the coldest evenings. They're sold at housewares stores but are also available for rent.

O Does the house smell good? Do you have an aromatic candle lit? (An alternative to scented candles is to light incense in a planter near the entrance or front door. Freesia incense placed among the flowers heightens the aromas.) If you don't like scented candles, at least put one in your bathroom.

O How's the lighting? Use dimmers, lamps, and candles to set just the right mood.

O Is music playing? When I plan a party, people always ask me to choose the music. Bad music is a surefire way to ruin a great party. If music isn't your thing, ask a friend who loves music to pick out something for you. World music is ideal because it's atmospheric and upbeat. Standards are always a good idea. Load up your iPod in advance so you can just plug it in and groove or tune in to satellite radio or the music station on cable television, which plays hours of music without commercials. I also like to create playlists using Pandora.com, a Web site that has almost every song imaginable and is easy to use. Play upbeat music no matter what—play old Pink Floyd only if you want your guests to go home!

Remember, it's the little things that really matter.

LULU'S FAVORITE COCKTAIL PARTY MUSIC

The Best of Cannonball Adderly
Herb Alpert and the Tijuana Brass
Maurice Chevalier
Stan Getz
Billie Holiday
Elton John
Diana Krall
Pink Martini
Frank Sinatra
World music (such as reggae, French, Arabic, African,
Armenian, or Brazilian—Putumayo World Music has
a great selection; see Sources)

CREATE A MOOD WITH SPACE

Keep the bar in an area where you want guests to congregate, to prevent people from spreading out everywhere. Shut off space by closing doors to encourage guests to remain in one area. Smaller spaces make parties look livelier—turn the music up a little to keep up with loud voices. At a Grammy party I threw a few years ago, we kept the doors closed for the first hour or two to keep guests in one room and make it look more crowded until more people showed up; then we threw open the doors to accommodate the growing crowd. At another client's home, we needed to clear out her living room to seat thirty-two people for dinner. My solution was to set up the living room outdoors, since the house had French doors leading outside. We rented space heaters to keep the guests warm and filled the area with candles, and it looked great.

Creating a bar/lounge atmosphere at a party is easy if you rent the right tables. Ask for pedestal tables (sometimes called bistro tables), which are extra-tall tables that people can crowd around and lean on. These tables are great for big parties because they create more space for guests to put their drinks on. Rent bar stools or stools with backs on them; ask the rental company for its advice about choosing the right stool. (Be sure to rent matching tablecloths, too.)

THE PARTY PANTRY

Pantries can be your best friend: they contain all the essentials to entertain at the last minute, no matter who drops by. The items on this list don't include staples like flour, sugar, salt, and pepper. The list shows what I keep in my pantry, but you should stock yours according to your taste and preferences. Trust me; a well-stocked pantry pays off.

Besides food, every entertaining kitchen needs a few basic items: one good, sharp chef's knife; a bread knife (which has many uses, from slicing bread to cutting tomatoes); a set of cheese knives; and a sauté pan.

Nice-to-have items include a grill pan and at least four rimmed baking sheets, the number you'll need for a party. (You can also buy disposable aluminum pans to transport food and to mix ingredients. Just recycle them after the party so there's no storage issue.)

If you have the storage space, stock up on assorted plates and bowls for serving. Pick them up when you see them on sale at flea markets, tag sales, or outlet stores. Don't forget that some upscale grocery stores sell serving dishes, so if you're pressed for time, just buy them while you're grocery shopping.

Lulu's Tip

I like to fill old glass jars with sugar and place a vanilla bean, orange peel, rosemary sprigs, or lavender buds in them. It takes about one week for the sugar to retain the flavors. I sprinkle the flavored sugar on top of shortbread, bake with it, or serve it with coffee or tea.

Herb Primer

I use fresh herbs in almost everything I make—they're easy to find and versatile. Some of my favorites are cilantro, mint, basil, lavender, and rosemary. Remove the leaves from the stems and add the herbs toward the end of cooking so they retain their full flavor.

O Bunches of fresh herbs will last up to two weeks in the refrigerator if you store them properly. Wrap them in a paper towel and place them in a sealed Tupperware container. The one exception is basil: it will last longer if you keep the bunch upright in a glass of water on the counter. If you have leftover herbs, puree them with a little olive oil (and garlic if you like) and pour the mixture into ice cube trays. Keep the herb cubes in your freezer and pop them in a dish when you need them.

O Fresh herbs are more intense in flavor than dried but contain mostly water, so you'll use a larger quantity of fresh than dried. (The standard substitution is 1/3 teaspoon powdered or 1 teaspoon crushed dried herbs for every tablespoon of chopped fresh herbs.)

O I also love to make my own herb-infused oils, which make a good substitute if you can't get fresh herbs. Simply combine 2 cups olive oil, 5 cloves chopped garlic, 2 stalks fresh rosemary, a handful of mint leaves, a handful of basil leaves, and 2 tablespoons salt in a saucepan. (Add hot red pepper flakes or whole dried chiles if you want a spicier oil.) As soon as the mixture boils, reduce the heat and simmer for 5 minutes. Turn off the heat and let the oil cool. Strain the oil into a pitcher. Using a funnel, pour the strained oil into a clean, empty water or wine bottle. It will last for months stored in the refrigerator. Bring to room temperature before using.

O It's simple to grow your own herbs year-round in small pots— you don't need a big garden to have a nice selection. On my kitchen windowsill, I keep pots of basil, rosemary, thyme, and mint and snip off leaves as needed.

The Complete Party Pantry List

This list of impromptu party staples includes everything you need for a last-minute cocktail or dinner party (in addition to what you've stocked the freezer with).

- Honey
- Olive oil
- Infused oils, such as chili oil
- Small jar mayonnaise
- Mustard
- Hot chili sauce (available in the international section of the grocery store or in any ethnic market)
- Jar of green olives
- Red pepper spread or tapenade (Make your own dip by adding mayonnaise to the tapenade. Any kind of tapenade will do, from green or black olive to red pepper.)
- Pesto, jarred (tomato, basil, or artichoke)
- Tabasco sauce
- Canned stewed tomatoes
- Jarred tomato sauce
- Harissa (a spicy red pepper paste available in the international section of most grocery stores)
- Salt (sea salt, such as Maldon; also see "Salt Primer," page 26)
- Ground black pepper (or invest in a pepper mill and use peppercorns)
- Dried herbs: cilantro, parsley, dill, rosemary, and basil (to garnish dishes, which makes things look homemade; see "Herb Primer," page 21)
- Garlic salt
- Lawry's Seasoned Salt
- Brown sugar
- Wasabi peas
- Potato chips
- Tortilla chips
- Jarred salsa
- Crackers (I prefer rice, but any type will do)
- Cheese sticks
- Roasted nuts or raw almonds
- Bag of whole peanuts, salted or unsalted (not just for snacking but to put in a cut-glass vase with branches or flowers and use as a centerpiece; you can also use pink lentils or green split peas for this)
- Artichoke hearts (canned or jarred)
- Can of chickpeas
- Instant risotto
- Box of penne and/or spaghetti
- Smoked fish, tuna, anchovies, or salmon (Serve with bowls of sour cream, sliced bread, and lemon wedges.)
- Cornichons
- Peanut butter and/or almond butter
- Graham crackers
- Dried apricots
- Box of red licorice

Most supermarkets these days are stocked for one-stop shopping, from hummus to fresh bread and wine, making impromptu parties a breeze.

- Bags of candy: M&M's, malt balls, chocolate bars (I prefer a good dark chocolate, such as Vosges; you can just break off pieces and serve that as dessert.)
- Hershey's Kisses
- Marshmallows
- Chocolate-covered raisins or nuts
- Chocolate wafers (Layer the wafers on a plate with fresh whipped cream for a quick version of an icebox cake.)
- Baking chocolate in individually wrapped 1-ounce squares
- Cake mix (chocolate or vanilla)
- Jell-O instant pudding mix
- Brownie mix
- Brownie bites (available in most supermarket bakeries, and a very simple, affordable dessert served with whipped cream; you can keep the brownies in the freezer too.)
- Jar of caramel
- Bag of chocolate chips
- Box of shortbread (Dip them in chocolate or crush them in a food processor and make a piecrust. Or dip them in melted caramel and a bowl of melted chocolate and serve as a quick dessert.)

- Box of good-quality cookies or toffee (easy to put out with a cup of coffee)
- Bisquick
- Mexican hot cocoa mix
- Containers of lemonade and iced tea mixes
- Tea bags
- Can of coffee and small can of decaf coffee
- Box of shelf-stable milk, such as Parmalat (in case you don't drink milk but a guest does)
- Coke and Diet Coke
- Ginger ale
- Pellegrino or club soda
- Wine (red and white)
- Beer
- Bottle of vodka
- Cassis (to pour over ice cream, fruit, or mix with yogurt)

See page 28 for a complete list of bar essentials.

Freezer Essentials

Whether it's pigs in a blanket or a great pizza, stocking the freezer is an important part of being prepared.

Nonperishables

These are the essentials I stock in my pantry, but feel free to add your favorites.

- Frozen cookie dough
- 1 can limeade
- 1 pint ice cream in any flavor (Serve with chocolate syrup and whipped cream in a can for an easy dessert.)
- Edamame
- Pizza dough
- Puff pastry (I use Pepperidge Farm.)
- Spinach
- 1 bag shredded cheese (I like a four-cheese blend. Smoked Gouda is also versatile, for a quesadilla or a pizza, for example.)
- 2 cups grated Parmesan
- Garlic butter (Store it in a Ziploc bag, just defrost it, and add to any pasta. Add any herbs you like.)
- A frozen pizza (Find a favorite pizza that you can put in your freezer or make your own with tortillas, sauce, and cheese; wrap and freeze. My favorite frozen pizza is Trader Joe's Alsatian pizza, a thin-crust pizza made with ham, which I top with truffle salt.)
- Flour tortillas
- Tomato sauce
- Grapes (Frozen grapes make a great garnish for drinks; see page 53.)
- Bananas (sliced)
- Sliced baguette

- Cocktail napkins (Buy a rubber stamp and stamp your initial(s) or address on the napkin if you don't want to spend a ton of money on customized napkins.)
- Heavy paper or disposable plates (preferably in a fun color; see Sources)
- Aromatic candles
- Toothpicks
- Squeeze bottles
- Extra trays
- Extra glassware
- Plastic cups
- Popsicle sticks
- Deli paper
- Plastic wrap (My favorite is Stretch-Tite; it clings and keeps things sealed.)
- Six matching bowls (or three of one kind and three of another)

How to Dress Up Leftovers

The more parties you throw, the more leftovers you may have. My refrigerator is often full of leftovers, and I've learned that I can make a meal out of anything. Follow your instincts and go for it—what's the worst that can happen? If you make a mistake and dinner is ruined, you can pull something from your freezer instead.

My go-to ingredient is citrus: lemons and limes brighten flavors instantly. Sprinkling on chopped fresh herbs is another easy way to liven up leftovers. Adding more sauce is also a great trick. For a dish like eggplant Parmesan, extra sauce will give it moisture and additional flavor. Shred leftover chicken and make curried chicken salad served over a bed of greens with sliced mango or papaya. (I always put a squeeze of fresh lemon or lime juice with a pinch of salt over the fruit. A pinch of cayenne pepper will also add flavor.) Leftover mashed potatoes make great potato cakes for breakfast the next morning; just form them into patties and sauté in butter. I've used leftover salmon to make salmon cakes on many occasions.

Transform leftover strip steak into a quesadilla by sautéing chopped onion in butter and adding finely chopped steak. Add red pepper flakes if desired, along with bell peppers and/or tomatoes. Heat a flour tortilla and place it on a plate. Top the tortilla with the steak and onions, along with a handful of shredded cheese. Garnish with shredded lettuce or fresh herbs, and if you have leftover rice, add that as well. (Leftover rice benefits from a hint of Tabasco, a squeeze of lemon or lime, a dash of garlic oil, a teaspoon of soy sauce, and any veggies you want to throw in.) Now you've got quite a meal! I also love to make steak salad with leftover beef. I toss the reheated beef with sweet chili sauce and fresh lime juice and serve it over greens. I store my leftovers in Tupperware or Pyrex glass storage containers.

Lulu's Tip

Mixing chicken stock with a little honey and freshly squeezed lemon or orange juice will rescue any overcooked chicken. Just pour the stock mixture over sliced chicken and serve any extra sauce on the side with a spoon. If you overcook steak, mix a little beef broth, a little red wine, and a little balsamic vinegar in a saucepan and boil for a minute for an instant sauce. Add a pinch of rosemary if you like.

Salt Primer

One of my favorite flavoring elements, besides maple syrup, is salt. These days there are so many types of salt, and you can use different types depending on the dish. Salt is harvested around the world, and supermarket shelves feature salts from virtually every location imaginable, including France, Hawaii, and India. Both machine- and hand-harvested salts are available, but look for hand-harvested salt for the best quality. My friend Joni, a salt expert, describes salt by the texture: fine, coarse, and flaky. There are also colored salts, smoked salts, pickling salts, and roasted salts. Salt and chocolate are an unexpected pairing; many pastry chefs use French *fleur de sel* on their desserts, and I love caramels topped with salt or *fleur de sel*.

Stay away from iodized table salt; it has flavor that can come off in the food, although baking with it is fine. I always use kosher salt for cooking, to salt pasta water, and to season dressings. For edamame, I use flaky Maldon sea salt from Britain. Flavored salts, like truffle salt, finish a dish and add another layer of flavor to simple foods such as a fresh avocado or a bowl of macaroni and cheese. I love to sprinkle truffle salt over a bowl of edamame.

Salt will stay fresh indefinitely, so it's worth keeping several types in your pantry. The best way to season with salt is to pinch it and sprinkle it over the food; you have much more control over the seasoning if you use your fingers.

STOCKING THE BAR

Unless you're having just a few people over, you should set up a bar for every party so that people can help themselves or refill their own drinks. I usually set up a bar area in my kitchen or in the dining area, with drinks, glasses, and ice. You can customize your bar as well: set up a Bloody Mary bar for a Sunday brunch or a make-your-own-martini bar for a cocktail party.

If you entertain often, it's good to have bar essentials on hand. When you're stocking the bar, remember what your friends drink when they come over. We have friends who drink only Negronis, so we always have the ingredients on hand. I happen to love Kir Royales, so I always have Champagne and Chambord, a raspberry liqueur, in my cabinet.

Don't forget garnishes! Festive touches like orange slices, gardenias, edible gold flakes, and even pickled vegetables look great in a glass—just use your imagination.

For a nonalcoholic drink, spear frozen grapes on toothpicks to mimic the olives that usually garnish a martini. Fruit is always a good choice, as well as a rosemary sprig, fresh dill or mint, or even a radish.

Bar snacks are a must. Everyone loves a nibble while waiting for a drink, whether sweet or savory: wasabi peas, roasted nuts, potato chips, cheese doodles, pretzels, popcorn, Cheez-Its, pistachios (with a bowl for the shells), Goldfish crackers, jelly beans, malt balls, mini Milano cookies—whatever you choose, make it fun. As a general rule, serve whatever you would enjoy. Even if you're not a snacker, you should put snacks out for your guests.

Popcorn makes a great bar snack, particularly as you can customize the flavors: add truffle oil or truffle butter, seasonings (like Cheddar seasoning, available at gourmet markets and online), sautéed garlic, homemade bacon bits (avoid canned), chopped fresh herbs such as rosemary or sage, or flavored salts. Just coat the popcorn lightly in butter or a flavored olive oil before adding the salt and/or herbs. For a decadent— and unforgettable—bar snack, drizzle bacon fat over plain popcorn and garnish it with fresh bacon bits.

The Essentials

These are the basics for stocking a bar if you entertain. If you want the bare-bones bar, simply keep wine and beer on hand. You can buy small bottles (50-milliliter size) of liquor such as vodka, Chambord, and tequila so you don't get stuck with a whole bottle. But again, stock what you and your friends drink.

- O Six-pack beer
- O Wine (one bottle each red and white)
- O Champagne or sparkling wine
- O Six-pack of canned cranberry juice
- O Six-pack of Coca-Cola and Diet Coke
- O Vodka
- O Gin
- O Rum (light)
- O Club soda
- O Tonic water (you can buy in small bottles if you prefer)

Flavored Vodka

It's good to keep at least one bottle of flavored vodka on hand for entertaining. I love Absolut Citron and use it to make my favorite drink, Tina's Tango (fresh lemon martini, page 170), a blend of fresh lemon juice, Absolut Citron, and Patrón Citrónge, a specialty liqueur. Keep in mind that there are various quality levels of vodka, and if you're using vodka only as a mixer you can buy the less expensive brands, as people cannot taste the difference once it's mixed. If you're serving only vodka and one other beverage, however, or setting up a martini bar, buy more expensive, premium vodka.

The Complete Bar

This is the powerhouse bar for when you want to have everything for everyone. You're the best judge of what you and your friends enjoy, so when stocking your bar, buy what you think you'll need, even if it's not on these lists.

- Vodka
- Gin
- Whisky
- Scotch
- Tequila (one bottle silver, one aged)
- Rum (one bottle silver, one dark)
- Jack Daniel's
- Dry vermouth
- Sweet vermouth
- Campari
- Bailey's Irish Cream
- Cognac
- Kahlúa
- Port
- Sambuca
- Amaretto
- Chambord
- Cachaça
- Chardonnay
- Sauvignon Blanc or Pinot Grigio
- Merlot or Pinot Noir
- Champagne or sparkling wine
- Heineken beer, Amstel Light beer
- Pellegrino or club soda
- Evian
- Tonic water
- Coca-Cola
- Diet Coke
- Sprite, 7UP, or ginger ale
- Rose's lime juice
- Margarita mix
- Margarita salt
- Cranberry juice
- Orange juice
- Grapefruit juice
- Tomato juice
- Accoutrements: olives, cherries, lemons, limes, any pickled vegetable such as onions, and ice

Bar Tools

- Strainer
- Shaker
- Ice tongs
- Ice bucket
- Bottle opener
- Stirrers
- Cocktail bar spoons
- Citrus reamer or lemon/lime squeezer
- Bar measure (otherwise known as a jigger)
- Cocktail napkins
- Cocktail picks
- Small straws (nice to have but not essential)
- Blender (nice to have but not essential)

ING

Entertaining in the morning is not as hard as you think (especially with a good cup of coffee in hand). Most breakfast food can be made the night before, but even cooking the morning of the gathering doesn't have to be overwhelming. Morning parties are the best way to get your feet wet if you're nervous about entertaining, because people don't expect much for breakfast. Unlike at a lunch or dinner, all many people want in the morning is a great cup of coffee or a glass of freshly squeezed juice.

Nothing gets me out of bed faster in the morning than the divine smell of my husband Stevie's rich, thick, always delicious coffee. I get up, put the kettle on, and take our dogs, Sweet Pea and Mr. Pickles, out for their morning walk.

Stevie makes his way to the kitchen, spooning just the right amount of Peet's French Roast coffee into a coffee press. While he waits for the water to boil, he fills the little copper pan we brought back from Armenia with organic whole milk and heats it on low. When the kettle bellows, he pours the water into the coffee cups, warming them up until the coffee is ready. Watching Stevie prepare the coffee is watching a master at work.

Besides a great cup of coffee, it's nice to offer some comforting breakfast foods. Use the buffet approach to get over any fear you may have about entertaining. For a truly impromptu morning party, run out and buy everything already made—including bakery items from your favorite local bakery and brewed coffee, which you can get in a box from stores like Whole Foods, Starbucks, Peet's Coffee, and Dunkin' Donuts—and just arrange it all on platters. Feel free to mix and match the recipes from the parties in this book, depending on the crowd you're serving and your own personal preference.

My husband and I like to eat toast with almond butter and a thin layer of jam. But growing up, breakfast meant piles of bacon, soft-boiled eggs, plates of scones, and orange juice—my mom cooked breakfast to order every day. With six kids in the family, there was a lot of hustle and bustle in the morning, from my older sisters blow-drying their hair in the bathroom to the smell of freshly baked muffins coming from the kitchen. While my sisters quickly left the house without breakfast, my brother and I waited for the blueberry muffins. I would sit down at the beautifully set table (my mother believed meals should be appreciated), drink my orange juice, and take my vitamins (which I sometimes disposed of in my napkin). My mom used her nice plates every day, as well as crystal and silver on Sundays, showing us that you don't have to save them for a special occasion. ("Saving" nice dishes is kind of like keeping your furniture covered in plastic!) There's always a reason to bring out your best stuff, even for burger night. Our holiday breakfasts were elaborate spreads—my parents prepared bacon, baked beans, platters of scrambled eggs or eggs fried to order, and mugs of hot chocolate, while the table was set with my mother's fine china and decorated with the Christmas cookies that the Powers clan had decorated.

Because my mom made breakfast delicious and lovely whether it was a Tuesday morning or a holiday celebration, breakfast was very social in our house. Our neighbors' kids would often come over before school and eat breakfast with us. Why? Because my mom made breakfast fun, delicious, and lovely. That's why I love to throw my doors open to friends and family for morning parties: *mi casa es tu casa*.

Even the busiest people with kids can stop by for a morning gathering. Don't think that kids will ruin a party; well-behaved kids add a certain energy to a gathering, and if you don't have kids, be a sport and go to a ninety-nine-cent or dollar store and get a few toys for them to play with. You can find so many little things that they'll love, and you'll look like a hero.

COFFEE AND NEWSPAPER PARTY

A cup of coffee is one of the best things about the morning, along with copies of your favorite newspapers—so why not celebrate it with friends? This party is easy to throw together in a few hours the day before. I start off with a trip to the local newsstand and buy newspapers from several cities, as well as a few tabloids for fun (otherwise known as my "periodicals")! It's entertaining made simple and a lot of fun. Whenever I throw a brunch like this, I find that everyone really starts talking about world events and reading from the papers and starting friendly debates, which makes it like a morning roundtable.

Living in southern California, we do a lot of our entertaining indoors/outdoors, meaning that guests can easily move from the kitchen to the outside table or patio. I put all the papers out in my courtyard on a low glass table or in the living room on the coffee table. (It's a good idea to provide towelettes or hand wipes to keep the newsprint at bay. Place

them in a bowl for easy access.) Also leave the latest copies of *Vogue, Vanity Fair,* and *Real Simple* laid out for guests to browse through. And I always put out a backgammon set—my husband is a backgammon fanatic, and not everyone reads the paper! If I'm expecting tons of kids, I place stacks of plain white paper or butcher paper, crayons, and coloring books on a low table or cover a small, low table in butcher paper with a pot of crayons so they can doodle at will. You can even hold a drawing contest for the kids.

I set up the kitchen like a bed-and-breakfast, inspired by my favorite B&B, the Simpson House in Santa Barbara, by putting a big cutting board over my sink to create one long counter so my guests can eat at their leisure. (You can really get ideas wherever you go. If you see something you like, whether it's a table centerpiece or a napkin fold, borrow it!) I make a pot of decaf and place it in a Thermos or insulated coffee-pot, and then I start the regular coffee. I always include a nice selection of tea bags (including herbal tea) and a pot of hot water (I love electric kettles that boil water in under a minute). Pitchers of orange or grape-fruit juice are a must. If you have a juicer, all the better. Leave it out on the counter with a bowl of oranges and grapefruits cut in half and let guests juice their own. And don't forget a pitcher of water. I like to set a bowl of mini muffins (store-bought or homemade) alongside. To me, this spread says, "Welcome! Come in and grab a drink." I always have juice boxes and chocolate syrup on hand to satisfy children's cravings.

Casual, homey food is easy: stick a toaster out on the kitchen counter along with potato bread, corn bread, bagels, butter, and jams so that guests can toast when and what they want. Consider leaving a bowl of eggs on the stove next to a frying pan, along with little bowls of garnishes like grated cheese, spinach, chopped scallions, and diced ham, allowing your guests to become their own egg masters. But come up with your own signature egg mixture—I mix up Boursin cheese and fresh herbs and add it to scrambled eggs, and it's become my standard break-

fast dish. To eliminate morning party madness, I make Mini Blueberry Pancakes (page 42) the night before and reheat them in the oven.

Leave the utensils and plates stacked in the kitchen so people can help themselves. Making bacon and sausage in the oven is a snap (and cuts down on cleanup), and I just set them both on top of the stove to stay warm. I also lay out a platter of smoked salmon with capers, thinly sliced tomato and red onion, whipped scallion cream cheese, and bagels, with mini bagels for the kids, which are available at most grocery stores. (Leftover mini bagels also make great dog treats; see page 167.) Set the salt and pepper shakers out, squeeze a few lemons on top of the salmon, lay out some lemon wedges, and serve a bottle of Tabasco on the side for those who want a kick.

> ## Lulu's Tip
>
> If you're using ceramic platters to serve food, heat them in a 200°F oven so the food stays warm. Alternatively, run them under very hot water and then dry them off. The same is true for coffee or tea servers.

My friend Todd eats in courses, and a lot of them—he is forever famished. At my house he starts with a toasted bagel with all the fixings, followed by fruit and muffins, and finally, his own "Todd's special" scrambled eggs. I love that—you want your guests to feel as comfortable as Todd does. And he's the ultimate guest; he calls me on his way to my parties to see if I need anything, and he always helps me clean up!

Invite guests for a two-hour period, say from 9:00 to 11:00 A.M. or 10:00 A.M. to noon. This way your guests can set their own pace, and you should be able to sit back, relax, and visit with your friends without running around like a chicken with your head cut off.

Morning Shortcuts: What's great about this party is that you can *buy* almost everything if you're short on time: scones, muffins, or croissants from a local bakery (or even a box of doughnut holes) and fruit salad from the market (just garnish with fresh mint).

If you want to prep the night before, set out a tray with coffee carafes, mugs, sugar, tea bags, lemon wedges, and brown sugar.

Morning Prep: That morning, fill a glass jar or small pitcher (whatever you have around the house that can double as a pitcher; it doesn't have to have a spout) with milk and put out serving trays, glasses, utensils, and any platters or baskets you're planning to use. A fun addition to the coffee or tea service are rock-sugar sticks or honey sticks (see Sources). It's also nice to put out a pitcher of simple syrup to sweeten tea, both hot and iced (see page 57).

DECORATING IDEAS

✳ A fun and unique way to lay out silverware is to wrap it in newspaper. Roll the silverware in a napkin in a square of newspaper and secure with a rubber band. (Newspapers can also double as tablecloths if you use double-sided tape—just cover the tabletop with newspapers and secure with tape.) Leave some wipes out. If you can find them, pick up wax paper bags with a newsprint design, available at some grocery stores.

* Use any type of glassware to hold utensils—juice glasses, small vases, or terra-cotta pots—or place the silverware in flowerpots, using a Sharpie or paint pen (available at art supply stores) to write on the flowerpots KNIVES, FORKS, and so on. Or place a piece of masking tape on the pot and write on the tape. One big terra-cotta pot filled with paper napkins also looks fabulous on a table.

* Fill a big wooden bowl with little cereal boxes and place it in the middle of the table for a fun morning centerpiece.

* Instead of laying the newspapers flat on a table, hang them over a rack to make them easy for guests to grab. Run a length of clothesline or heavy twine across the backyard or in the living room and drape the newspapers over it. A magazine rack is also great for this, and even a clothes-drying rack would work (wood or metal, available at most housewares stores). (To add some extra flourish, decorate the drying rack by wiring some gerbera daisies to it!)

Lulu's Tip

I always leave my butter out on the counter the night before a party so it can soften. (Please don't put out cold butter for your guests.) I often make my own flavored butters. Honey butter is one of my favorites. It's a cinch to make and divine on bread. Simply combine one stick of softened butter with a few tablespoons of honey. Orange butter is delicious on pancakes—just blend a teaspoon of fresh orange zest with your stick of butter. Or make strawberry butter by adding tablespoons of strawberry jam. Savory butters, which some people call *hotel butters,* are also easy to make; mix butter with roasted garlic or chopped fresh herbs. Use your imagination to create whatever fun butters you can think of. And remember, there's no wrong way to do it—you're the chef!

The Lowdown on Java

I adore coffee, but making a good pot takes a few tricks. I like the intensity of coffee made using a French press (see below).

Start off with freshly ground beans, whether ground at the store or at home. (Even when I travel I bring my own beans.) To keep your coffee hot longer, try a trick I learned from my neighbor Bella: pour hot water into the mug to warm it while the coffee is brewing.

Another special touch for coffee is steamed milk. First heat it in a pan or microwave and then use an inexpensive, battery-operated frother to whip it up (see Sources). It takes just minutes and will really impress your guests. (If there's one trick you get from this book, it should be to warm your milk! Who wants to throw cold milk into a cup of hot coffee?) After you've added the froth or warm milk, dust the top with cinnamon or grated chocolate to look like a true pro.

Don't throw out leftover coffee; there are many uses for it. Pour it into an old jelly or pickle jar and make iced coffee for an afternoon pick-me-up. I like iced coffee two ways: made with milk and ice or with my favorite, vanilla ice cream. Or, for a total indulgence, make adult milk shakes with leftover coffee and coffee ice cream and a splash of Bailey's. For a lighter treat, freeze coffee in small paper cups to make your own coffee Popsicles. You can also use leftover coffee to make the classic Italian dessert *affogato*—a scoop of ice cream with coffee (traditionally espresso) poured over the top.

Don't toss the grounds! Over the years I've come up with endless uses for them. Fill a clean old sock with coffee grounds, secure it with a rubber band, and use it to eliminate odors in the freezer, refrigerator, or microwave. Mix coffee grounds with soap to scrub away any cooking odors on your hands. My favorite hand scrub—I call it my coffee salve—consists of coffee grounds mixed with hand soap. I also combine coffee grounds and honey to make a body scrub for the shower. My friends say it should be bottled!

HOW TO MAKE FRENCH-PRESS COFFEE

In the morning I use the large (16-ounce) French press so I can use any leftover coffee for iced coffee or reheat it for a late morning cup.

① Buy freshly ground beans or grind your own. Start with 3 rounded tablespoons of ground coffee per cup of coffee.

② Bring a kettle of water to a boil. Let cool for 40 seconds.

(3) Add the water to the press and fill three-quarters full. Quickly stir the grounds with a long spoon. Fit the top just over the top of the press (don't press down yet) and let the coffee steep for 2 to 3 minutes. If you want a stronger European-style coffee, mix one part coffee to one part water.

(4) Gently press the filter top and plunge it down. Pour the coffee into coffee cups.

My favorite coffee idea for dinner parties is serving little individual presses that you can buy for around two dollars each at IKEA. It looks very chic to carry out a tray with individual pots of coffee. Of course, French presses aren't just for making coffee; they can be used to serve gazpacho or hot soup or for brewing a pot of loose tea. (If you're making coffee in the small presses, use 2 heaping tablespoons of ground coffee per press and up to 4 tablespoons if you like it strong.)

COFFEE SALVE

½ cup coffee grounds
½ cup liquid hand soap
   (any variety will do)
2 tablespoons honey (optional)

Mix all the ingredients and place the salve in a glass jar. It's great to keep on the kitchen counter.

LULU'S BODY SCRUB

This everyday scrub will keep for up to 1 month.

½ cup coffee grounds
¼ cup Epsom salts
½ cup honey
1 teaspoon eucalyptus oil (available at health food stores)
1 teaspoon lavender oil (available at health food stores)

Mix all the ingredients and place the scrub in a glass jar.

Cheesy Scrambled Eggs

SERVES 4

When I first ate these eggs, I thought there was some secret ingredient that made them taste so incredible. My sister Julie told me the secret was in the cheese. She uses Laughing Cow brand cheese triangles, making them the best cheesy scrambled eggs you'll ever taste. I like to add flavorings to my scrambled eggs, such as salsa, sautéed onions, fresh chives, or whatever else is in my fridge. Good scrambled eggs take a little time, but the most important thing is not to overcook them. Adding a little extra liquid helps prevent this.

2 tablespoons unsalted butter or olive oil
8 large eggs
Salt and freshly ground pepper to taste
3 to 4 triangles (from a 6-ounce package) Laughing Cow brand cheese

1. Place a medium skillet, preferably nonstick, over medium heat for about 1 minute. Add the butter or olive oil and swirl it around the pan.

2. Meanwhile, crack the eggs into a bowl and beat them just until the yolks and whites are combined. Season with salt and pepper and beat in 2 tablespoons water.

3. Add the eggs to the skillet and turn the heat to medium-low. As the eggs begin to set, add the cheese and stir often, scraping the eggs from the bottom of the pan, until the cheese is melted and the eggs are no longer runny.

4. Serve immediately.

VARIATIONS: Two of my favorite scrambled egg combinations are goat cheese and fresh herbs and Gruyère, ham, parsley, and pear. I also love to add a spoonful of my own herb cheese, based on the Boursin brand (see page 41).

Lulu's Boursin Cheese

This is my absolute favorite recipe from childhood. Spread it on basically anything, from bread and crackers to veggies and Granny Smith apple slices. This keeps for 1 week in the refrigerator.

MAKES 2 CUPS

2 garlic cloves

¼ cup packed fresh flat-leaf parsley

¼ cup packed fresh dill

¼ cup packed fresh chives

½ cup shredded Swiss cheese

One 8-ounce package cream cheese, at room temperature

1 teaspoon sugar

1 tablespoon lemon zest

1 tablespoon freshly squeezed lemon juice

1 tablespoon Tabasco sauce

1 teaspoon salt

½ teaspoon white pepper

2 tablespoons vegetable oil

In the bowl of a food processor, combine the garlic and herbs and pulse until combined. Add the remaining ingredients and blend until smooth. Keep in the refrigerator and bring to room temperature before serving.

Mini Blueberry Pancakes

I made these for the noontime commitment ceremony of my friends Kerry and Karen. You can also serve these as a passed appetizer with sliced banana, powdered sugar, and a dollop of syrup.

SERVES 10

1 cup all-purpose flour

1 tablespoon sugar

2 tablespoons baking powder

¼ teaspoon salt

1 large egg, beaten

1 teaspoon vanilla extract

1 cup milk

3 tablespoons canola or other neutral-flavored cooking oil

1 pint fresh blueberries or 2 cups frozen

1. In a mixing bowl, stir together the flour, sugar, baking powder, and salt. In another mixing bowl, combine the egg, vanilla, milk, and 2 tablespoons of the oil. Add the egg mixture to the flour mixture all at once. Stir just until blended but still slightly lumpy.

2. Pour the batter into a squeeze bottle.

3. Lightly grease a griddle or heavy skillet with the remaining 1 tablespoon oil and heat over medium-high heat.

4. Squeeze the batter onto the griddle, forming silver dollar–size circles, and set a few berries into each pancake.

5. Cook the pancakes until the edges begin to brown and bubbles form on top, 1 to 2 minutes. Flip and cook until golden brown, another minute or so.

6. Serve hot with a pitcher of syrup, a pitcher of melted butter, and some powdered sugar. The pancakes are also delicious with a piece of bacon on top.

NOTE: You can make these ahead and freeze them: cool the pancakes completely, layer them with deli paper, tinfoil, or wax paper, and wrap tightly in plastic wrap or seal in a Tupperware container.

Maple-Glazed Bacon

Almost everyone loves bacon, and this recipe improves on it, if that's even possible! When I make this recipe, I end up eating half the bacon, and, if my husband Stevie wanders into the kitchen, which he does every 10 minutes, it's gone before I can even put it on a plate. So if you're like us, do yourself a favor and make extra. If you have leftover bacon, wrap it in deli paper, put it in the fridge, and reheat it the next day in a frying pan, or use it in BLT sandwiches.

SERVES 6 TO 8

⅔ cup grade A or B maple syrup (not the fake stuff)

2 teaspoons Dijon mustard

¼ cup packed brown sugar

2 pounds beef, turkey, soy, or pork bacon

① Preheat the oven to 325°F.

② In a small, heavy saucepan, mix together the syrup, mustard, and sugar and cook over low heat, stirring often, until the syrup thickens, about 10 minutes. If you're pressed for time, mix together the syrup, mustard, and sugar in a mixing bowl and brush it on the cooked bacon. Set aside.

③ Fry the bacon in a large pan over medium-high heat, and if you have one, use a bacon weight to keep the bacon flat as it cooks.

④ When the bacon is cooked to your liking, drain it on a paper towel. Lay the flattened bacon on a jelly-roll pan and brush the glaze on both sides. Don't place the bacon on paper towels, because it will stick to the paper. Use a baking pan or serving pan.

⑤ Bake for 10 to 12 minutes. Serve hot.

NOTE: To eliminate the extra grease, you can cook the bacon in the oven on a cooling rack placed in a jelly-roll pan. The grease will fall onto the pan while the bacon cooks on the rack.

Smoked Salmon Platter

I love toasted poppy seed bagels with scallion cream cheese, a slice of red onion, a slice of tomato, smoked salmon, a squeeze of lemon, freshly ground pepper, and salt. I don't have it too often, but when I do I savor every bite. You can buy flavored whipped cream cheese or make your own.

SERVES 10 TO 12

3 medium tomatoes, thinly sliced
1 Bermuda or red onion, thinly sliced
1 small jar capers, drained
1 lemon, cut into wedges
1½ pounds smoked salmon or lox

Whipped Scallion Cream Cheese
    (recipe follows)
2 dozen bagels
    (a variety of flavors and sizes)

Arrange the tomatoes, onion, capers, lemon, and smoked salmon on a large platter. Place a bowl of cream cheese in the middle of the platter and serve with a basket of bagels. Alternatively, place all the ingredients (except the bagels) in separate covered bowls. This is a great way to prep the night before so that the morning of the party you just have to pull out the bowls and place them next to the bagels.

NOTE: If you're cutting the tomatoes the night before, place them on paper towels to absorb any liquid.

Whipped Scallion Cream Cheese

You can buy prepared scallion cream cheese if you're short on time. This keeps for 1 week in the refrigerator.

MAKES 1 CUP

One 8-ounce package cream cheese, at room temperature
1 teaspoon grated lemon zest
¼ cup thinly sliced scallion, both white and green parts

(1) Whip the cream cheese until fluffy in a mixer with the whip attachment or with a hand mixer.

(2) Add the lemon zest and scallion and mix well.

Mini Turkey Breakfast Patties

One morning I went over to my neighbor Shula's to borrow some milk. Shula cooks a big Shabbat dinner every week, and on that Friday she happened to be making turkey sausages that smelled scrumptious. I had never thought of making turkey sausage patties. I took that idea home with me and created my own breakfast patties, which can even be used for lunch or dinner.

MAKES 20 TO 22 PATTIES, SERVING 10

1 pound ground dark turkey meat

1 teaspoon ground cumin

2 teaspoons Lawry's Seasoned Salt

½ teaspoon freshly ground black pepper

3 scallions, both white and green parts, finely chopped

¼ cup chopped fresh cilantro

½ teaspoon Tabasco sauce

1 tablespoon grade A or B maple syrup

1 small Granny Smith apple, cored and chopped, skin left on

½ cup finely chopped red onion

1 tablespoon fennel seeds

Juice of 1 lime

① Mix all the ingredients together in a large bowl.

② Form the mixture into 1-ounce patties.

③ Cook the sausages in a sauté pan over medium heat for 2 minutes on each side. Serve hot.

NOTE: You can prepare the patties in advance and freeze them in an airtight container. Let thaw in the fridge before cooking.

JUST AN IDEA: Serve the sausage patties as burgers accompanied by salad, potatoes, or veggies—whatever you desire.

Sugar-Crusted Raspberry Muffins

My father happened to love a sweet in the afternoon, and one day my mother made these muffins for him. He emailed the recipe to all my sisters and me, with the subject line "muffin recipe—out of this world."

When I bake these delicious muffins, I always set aside a few to stick in the freezer. If they're a day or two old, I cut them in half and toast them with a little butter, a little trick my dad taught me. Substitute other berries if you like, such as blueberries, blackberries, or strawberries, or combine all of them for mixed berry muffins. Frozen berries will also work.

MAKES 24 MUFFINS OR 48 MINI MUFFINS

1¾ cups all-purpose flour

1 cup sugar

2 teaspoons baking powder

1 teaspoon salt

1 tablespoon ground cinnamon

8 tablespoons (1 stick)
  unsalted butter, melted

1 cup milk

1 large egg

1 teaspoon vanilla extract

2 cups fresh raspberries

FOR THE TOPPING

1 cup sugar

1 teaspoon ground cinnamon

1. Preheat the oven to 400°F. Line two 12-cup muffin tins with paper liners or grease with cooking spray or butter.

2. For the muffins, combine the flour, sugar, baking powder, salt, and cinnamon in a medium bowl. Slowly stir in the melted butter.

3. Add the milk, egg, and vanilla and mix gently until combined. The batter will be lumpy. Carefully fold in the raspberries.

4. Spoon the batter into muffin cups, filling each half full. Fill any empty muffin tins with water.

5. For the topping, combine the sugar and cinnamon in a small bowl. Dust the top of the muffins with the topping.

6. Bake for 17 to 20 minutes (10 to 12 minutes if you're using tins for mini muffins). Set aside and let cool for 10 minutes.

Cinnamon Sensations

My friends' kids love to come to my house. Do you think it's because I have a counter filled with candy jars, or is it these yummy treats that I always have in my freezer? I think it's both. I call these my Cinnamon Sensations.

MAKES APPROXIMATELY 90 STICKS

1 1arge loaf white bread, thinly sliced
One 8-ounce package cream cheese,
  at room temperature
2 large egg yolks

1 cup sugar
½ pound (2 sticks) salted butter, melted
½ teaspoon ground cinnamon

① Line a baking sheet with a Silpat baking mat or parchment paper.

② Place the bread slices in a single layer on a piece of wax paper and carefully roll over them a few times with a rolling pin to flatten slightly. Cut off the crusts.

③ In a medium bowl, whisk the cream cheese, egg yolks, and ½ cup of the sugar. Spread the mixture on one side of each slice of bread. Roll up each slice of bread into a cigar shape and press the edge to secure the roll tightly.

④ Place the melted butter in a shallow bowl. Combine the remaining ½ cup sugar with the cinnamon in a separate shallow bowl.

⑤ Dip each roll into the melted butter and then coat with the sugar-cinnamon mixture. Place the rolls on the baking sheet and freeze for at least 4 hours. (You can freeze them at this point for up to 1 month; just wrap tightly in plastic wrap.)

⑥ Preheat the oven to 375°F and grease a baking sheet.

⑦ Slice each bread roll into 3 or 4 cigarlike pieces and place them on the baking sheet.

⑧ Bake the sticks for 8 to 10 minutes, rotating the pan once. They will be golden brown when done.

⑨ Serve the Cinnamon Sensations hot. (Reheat any leftovers in a 375°F oven for 5 minutes.)

Patty P's French Coffee Cake

When I was growing up in Connecticut, I knew it was either Sunday or a holiday when this cake was brought out. I always make one to eat immediately and another to stick in my freezer.

SERVES 12

FOR THE TOPPING
1 cup chopped walnuts or pecans
1 cup packed brown sugar
2 teaspoons ground cinnamon

FOR THE CAKE
8 tablespoons (1 stick) unsalted butter
8 tablespoons (1 stick) margarine
5 large eggs
¾ cup packed brown sugar
¾ cup granulated sugar

3 cups all-purpose flour
2 teaspoons baking powder
1 teaspoon baking soda
1 teaspoon salt
One 3-ounce package instant vanilla pudding mix
1 cup sour cream
2 teaspoons vanilla extract
1 teaspoon almond extract

1. Preheat the oven to 350°F and grease a tube pan or Bundt pan with nonstick cooking spray.

2. To make the topping, combine the nuts, brown sugar, and cinnamon in a small bowl.

3. For the cake, blend the butter and margarine together in a large bowl until light and fluffy. Add the eggs one at a time, beating well after each addition.

4. Whisk the sugars, flour, baking powder, baking soda, salt, and pudding mix together in a large bowl. Mix the dry ingredients into the butter-egg mixture and then add the sour cream and vanilla and almond extracts.

5. Pour half the batter into the tube pan or Bundt pan. Sprinkle half the topping over the batter. Add the remaining batter to the pan and sprinkle on the remaining topping.

6. Bake for 50 to 60 minutes, until a skewer or toothpick inserted in the middle of the cake comes out clean or the cake springs back when pressed gently with your finger.

7. Let the cake cool in the pan for at least 1 hour.

8. Remove the cooled cake from the pan and place it on a serving platter.

NOTE: This cake freezes well. Let it cool completely, wrap it in tinfoil, and freeze for up to 1 month. Thaw at room temperature.

BLOODY MARYS

Bloody Marys just hit the spot. Uncle John, my husband's grandfather, had one every night around 5:30 P.M. When we visited him in Palm Desert, I always agreed to have one so that he wouldn't think I was a pain, so I've come to love a good Bloody. I like to serve a variety of garnishes on a lazy Susan, including green olives, pickled onions, caper berries, celery sticks, lemon slices, and long, skinny carrots with their tops on (available at most grocery stores). Some like it hot and spicy and some not, so I've included two recipes to please everyone. Even without the alcohol, they're a staple weekend drink at our house.

Lulu's Bloody Mary—the Mild One

SERVES 2

1 cup Clamato tomato cocktail

½ teaspoon prepared horseradish

1 teaspoon Worcestershire sauce

½ teaspoon Tabasco sauce

¼ teaspoon Beau Monde seasoning
(available at most grocery stores)
or celery salt

Juice of ½ small lemon

5 twists freshly ground pepper

3 ounces lemon vodka

Put all the ingredients into a shaker filled with ice and shake for a minute to combine. Fill tall glasses with ice and add the Bloody Mary mixture.

Stevie's Bloody Mary—the Spicy One

SERVES 2

1 cup Clamato tomato cocktail

¼ teaspoon celery seeds

¼ teaspoon dill seeds

¼ teaspoon Beau Monde seasoning or
celery salt

1 teaspoon Tabasco sauce

½ teaspoon Worcestershire sauce

½ teaspoon prepared horseradish

Juice of ½ lime

3 ounces lemon vodka

¼ teaspoon Old Bay seasoning

Put all the ingredients into a shaker filled with ice and shake for a minute to combine. Fill tall glasses with ice and add the Bloody Mary mixture.

VARIATION: You could also add a splash of caper juice and garnish with a caper berry.

HOUSEGUEST BREAKFAST

Everyone has houseguests at some time or another! With any guests, a leisurely breakfast in the kitchen can be the best part of the day, talking over coffee and just enjoying the morning. When my husband and I visit our uncle Joe and auntie Joyce, she always has juice out as well as bacon and sliced papaya or melon adorned with fresh mint. I have to say it makes me feel special—we sit around the breakfast table and discuss just about everything.

It's nice to offer a variety of dishes to your houseguests, and if you can, ask them ahead of time what they like or if they have any allergies or dietary preferences (sugar versus Splenda, for example). If granola isn't hearty enough, you can always whip up some soft-boiled eggs and serve them with toast. Smoothies are easy to make and can be tailored to fit anyone's taste. The recipes that follow can all be made ahead, so you just have to arrange a few platters before collapsing on the couch the night before. If you do enjoy baking, I've included some of my favorite breakfast pastry recipes, which can also be made the night before (or can be frozen and reheated the next morning).

Don't feel as if you need to go overboard; most people are fine with cereal, toast, or fruit. Trust me—no one will expect anything elaborate. Your guests will appreciate that you got up, had the coffee and tea ready, and put out a pitcher of juice. Making the effort is 90 percent of it. You're making your guests feel welcome with just those little touches.

The Breakfast Pantry

When you don't have time to run to the store, it's great to have a few breakfast items on hand, such as jars of peanut butter or almond butter, a variety of jams, a variety pack of individual-sized cereals, and packets of instant oatmeal. I keep a loaf of bread in the freezer as well as packages of puff pastry and chocolate croissants. Or buy ready-made frozen croissants at Trader Joe's or Williams-Sonoma; some of them taste just as good as if you had bought them from your local bakery. Buy bags of frozen berries to throw into muffins or smoothies.

It is always good to keep some bananas on hand for cereal toppings, smoothies, or just a boost of potassium. (If no one ends up eating them, make a batch of Chocolate-Banana Bread (page 74) and freeze it or make mini banana muffins.)

Smoothies are an easy breakfast treat. I love adding maple- or vanilla-flavored goat's milk yogurt or Greek yogurt to my smoothies; it makes them thick and creamy. If your guests don't want or can't tolerate dairy, you can use fruit to thicken your smoothies. Fruits such as mango, papaya, and banana add a thickness to smoothies, and you can buy them fresh or already pureed. (I even use Odwalla premade smoothies and blend them with yogurt when I'm short on time; they taste just as good as homemade smoothies. My finicky husband, who claims to eat only fresh, organic fruit, never notices!) If you like a little crunch, add almonds, ground flax seed, or wheat germ (or all three)—it also boosts the health quotient.

You can keep grapes and even bananas in the freezer (just slice them, put the slices back in the banana stem, and toss into a freezer bag). I like to put frozen grapes in my wine, a habit I picked up from my father as a kid. My father would come in from his vegetable garden, pour a glass of wine, and adorn it with a red radish or frozen grapes, just to add flair to the drink (and keep it cold).

Lulu's Tip

It's always nice to put flowers around the house before overnight guests arrive, and flowers, a bottle of water, and even a note that says "welcome" on their bedside table.

Lulu's Granola

Serve this crunchy granola with vanilla or maple goat's milk yogurt, milk, and fresh fruit or even over ice cream. I love eating a bowl of granola with fruit as a snack in the middle of the day. It's also a great hostess gift. Buy pretty jars or bags and package your own, tied with a ribbon.

MAKES ABOUT 10 CUPS

3 cups old-fashioned rolled oats

1 cup unsweetened dried flaked coconut

2 teaspoons ground cinnamon

½ teaspoon freshly grated nutmeg

½ cup vegetable oil

½ cup plus 2 tablespoons honey

⅛ cup peanut oil

½ cup sugar

1 cup whole raw almonds

½ cup whole shelled walnuts

½ cup shelled pistachios

½ cup raw cashews

½ cup banana chips

½ cup dried cranberries

½ cup golden raisins

½ cup dried apricots, julienned

½ cup dried pineapple, chopped

½ cup candied ginger, chopped

① Preheat the oven to 300°F.

② In a large bowl, stir together the oats, coconut, cinnamon, and nutmeg.

③ In another bowl, stir together the vegetable oil and the ½ cup honey until well combined. Pour the mixture over the oats and toss to combine well.

④ Spread the mixture evenly on a baking sheet and bake, stirring frequently, until golden brown, about 50 minutes. Remove from the oven and let cool in the pan.

⑤ In a medium saucepan over medium-high heat, combine the peanut oil, the remaining 2 tablespoons honey, and the sugar. When the honey mixture dissolves and begins to turn a light caramel color, after 8 to 10 minutes, add the almonds, walnuts, pistachios, cashews, and banana chips, stirring to coat. Remove from the heat and spread the nut mixture on a Silpat or greased cookie sheet to cool completely.

⑥ Once the nut mixture has cooled, break it apart into pieces. (The nuts can also be served on their own as a delicious nut brittle.)

⑦ In a large bowl, combine the granola with the nuts, cranberries, raisins, apricots, pineapple, and ginger.

⑧ Store the cooled granola in a Ziploc bag or Tupperware container for up to 2 weeks.

Soft-Boiled Eggs

As a kid, my favorite breakfast was soft-boiled eggs. My mom put my eggs into little egg dishes, and I cracked them open myself with the back of my spoon, adding a little salt and pepper. Now, once a week my neighbor Bella makes me soft-boiled eggs while she gives me French lessons. She serves the eggs with matzoh she's toasted on her gas stove and fresh sweet cream butter. I love to dip the matzoh into the egg yolk. Later in life I discovered potato bread, and I love its sweet taste with the yolks, but use whatever bread you have on hand.

SERVES 4

8 large eggs
8 slices potato bread
Softened salted or unsalted butter to taste
Salt and pepper to taste

1. Bring a medium saucepan of water to a gentle boil over medium heat.

2. Carefully place the eggs in the water, cook for 3 to 4 minutes, and drain.

3. Run the eggs very briefly under cold water, crack the top part of each egg with the back of a spoon, and place it in an egg cup.

4. While the eggs are cooking, toast the potato bread and spread with butter.

5. Cut the toast into strips and serve warm with the soft-boiled eggs and salt and pepper.

Fruit Salad with Herb, Citrus, Mint-Maple, or Basic Syrup

When I was growing up, my mom would cut up fresh fruit and arrange it on a plate with a shot glass full of toothpicks. She would also toss fresh fruit with some orange or lime juice and sugar. Taking inspiration from her, I came up with my own version: lime, lemon, a little maple syrup, and an herb syrup with rosemary or mint.

Cut your fruit into chunks rather than into small pieces; I find that small pieces of fruit get mealy and mushy. Make the salad the morning you're going to serve it, but if you're determined to make it the night before, cut up the fruit, store it in separate containers, and then toss it together in the morning. Use whatever fruit you'd like (bananas, apples, berries—the possibilities are endless), but unless you're using the ripest, sweetest seasonal fruit, add a little sugar.

MAKES 10 CUPS

Fruit Salad

1 pint strawberries, hulled and halved

1 half-pint raspberries

1 half-pint blueberries or blackberries

2 oranges, peeled and cut into sections

2 kiwis, peeled and cut into large chunks

1 mango, peeled, pitted, and cut into large chunks

1 papaya, peeled, pitted, and cut into large chunks

2 cups fresh pineapple cut into large chunks

1 cup cantaloupe or honeydew melon cut into large chunks

¼ cup fresh mint, julienned

Syrup (recipes follow)

Fresh rosemary or mint sprigs if you're using Herb Syrup

Combine all the fruit in a large bowl and stir in one of the syrups. Garnish with the mint or rosemary sprigs if you're using Herb Syrup.

Herb Syrup

1 cup sugar
½ cup chopped fresh rosemary or mint

1. Bring 1 cup water to a boil in a small saucepan over low heat and add the sugar and herb. Boil until the sugar is completely dissolved, about 2 minutes.

2. Strain through a colander into a bowl.

3. Let the syrup cool and combine with the fruit.

4. Serve immediately or store for up to 1 month in the refrigerator.

Citrus Syrup

¼ cup orange juice
¼ cup freshly squeezed lime juice
2 tablespoons sugar

1. Combine the juices and sugar in a small saucepan and boil for 2 to 3 minutes over low heat.

2. Remove from the heat and let cool.

3. Pour the cooled syrup over the fruit or store for up to 1 month in the refrigerator.

Mint-Maple Syrup

1 cup fresh mint leaves
¼ cup grade A or B maple syrup

1. Bring 1 cup of water to a boil. Remove from the heat.

2. Add the mint and the maple syrup and let the mint steep for 15 minutes, until cool.

3. Strain and pour the syrup over the fruit or store for up to 1 month in the refrigerator.

Basic Simple Syrup

1 cup sugar

① Combine the sugar with ½ cup water in a small, heavy saucepan and bring to a boil.

② Boil until the sugar is completely dissolved, about 2 minutes. Pour over the fruit or store for up to 1 month in the refrigerator.

JUST AN IDEA: Add these syrups to your tea and cocktails. I've even poured rosemary syrup over roasted walnuts.

Alex's Chocolate Scones with Cinnamon Clotted Cream

I have six godchildren, and this recipe is from my eldest, Princess Killian, aka Alex, my sister Julie's oldest child. She loves to bake, and these are her specialty.

MAKES 8 TO 12 SCONES

2 cups all-purpose flour

⅓ cup plus 2 tablespoons sugar

2½ teaspoons baking powder

½ teaspoon salt

1½ cups coarsely chopped bittersweet or semisweet chocolate or milk chocolate chunks or a mixture of all three

1¼ cups plus 1 tablespoon heavy cream

1 teaspoon unsweetened cocoa powder

Cinnamon Clotted Cream (recipe follows)

① Position a rack in the center of the oven and preheat to 425°F. Line a baking sheet with a Silpat baking mat, a sheet of aluminum foil, or parchment sprayed with nonstick baking spray.

② In a mixer, mix the flour, the ⅓ cup sugar, the baking powder, and salt. Add the chopped chocolate and the cream. Mix just until the dry ingredients and the cream come together.

③ Gather the dough onto a lightly floured board and knead until the dough just holds together.

④ Gently press or roll the dough to a ¾-inch thickness and use a round cookie cutter or a glass to cut out the scones. Gather up the scraps of dough, roll them out, and cut out additional scones.

(5) Place the dough rounds at least 1 inch apart on the lined baking sheet.

(6) Mix the remaining 2 tablespoons of sugar with the cocoa powder. Using a pastry brush, brush the tops with the milk or cream and sprinkle lightly with the sugar-cocoa mixture.

(7) Bake the scones until the tops are golden brown, 10 to 15 minutes, depending on the size.

(8) Let the scones cool on a baking rack and serve warm or at room temperature with Cinnamon Clotted Cream.

NOTE: The scones can be frozen for up to 1 month, wrapped in plastic wrap.

Cinnamon Clotted Cream

You can also serve this cream on top of apple tarts, ice cream, any pie or cobbler, or in a cup of coffee.

MAKES 2 CUPS

1 cup heavy cream
1 tablespoon
   confectioners' sugar
1 tablespoon vanilla
   extract
1 teaspoon unsweetened
   cocoa powder
½ teaspoon ground
   cinnamon
½ cup sour cream

(1) Whip the cream, sugar, vanilla, cocoa powder, and cinnamon in a mixer or food processor until firm peaks form.

(2) Fold the sour cream into the mixture. Store in the refrigerator for up to 4 days.

Sticky Buns

One word: scrumptious! You'll be delighted.

MAKES 10 TO 12 BUNS

FOR THE DOUGH

¾ cup cottage cheese

⅓ cup buttermilk

¼ cup sugar

4 tablespoons (½ stick) unsalted butter, melted

1 teaspoon vanilla extract

2 cups all-purpose flour, plus flour for rolling

1 tablespoon baking powder

½ teaspoon salt

¼ teaspoon baking soda

FOR THE WALNUT FILLING

3 tablespoons unsalted butter, melted

¼ cup honey

½ cup granulated sugar

½ cup packed light or dark brown sugar

2 teaspoons ground cinnamon

¼ teaspoon pumpkin pie spice

1 cup finely chopped walnuts

FOR THE TOPPING

¼ cup packed dark brown sugar

¼ cup honey

¼ cup corn syrup

4 tablespoons (½ stick) unsalted butter

1 teaspoon ground cinnamon

⅛ teaspoon pumpkin pie spice

1 teaspoon freshly squeezed lemon juice

½ cup finely chopped walnuts or other nuts

① For the dough, combine the cottage cheese, buttermilk, sugar, melted butter, and vanilla in the bowl of a food processor and process until smooth, about 15 seconds.

② Add the flour, baking powder, salt, and baking soda and pulse in short bursts just until the dough comes together. The dough should be quite moist.

③ Place the dough on a floured surface. Rub your hands with flour and knead just until smooth; 4 to 6 times should be sufficient. Use a rolling pin to roll the dough into a 15 x 18-inch rectangle.

④ To make the filling, whisk the melted butter and honey together in a small mixing bowl. Brush the dough with the honey butter to within ½ inch of the edges.

5. Combine the sugars, cinnamon, pumpkin pie spice, and walnuts in a mixing bowl. Sprinkle half of the walnut mixture onto the buttered part of the dough. Press the mixture into the dough, being careful to maintain the dough's even thickness.

6. To make the topping, combine the brown sugar, honey, corn syrup, butter, cinnamon, pumpkin pie spice, and lemon juice in a saucepan over medium heat and cook until just melted. Remove from the heat and add the nuts. Set aside.

7. To assemble and bake: Preheat the oven to 400°F and grease the cups of a 12-cup muffin tin with cooking spray.

8. Roll up the dough, starting with a long edge. Seal the seam by pinching it and then roll it so that the seam is on the bottom, leaving the ends open.

9. Using a sharp knife, slice the roll into 10 to 12 uniform pieces.

10. Cut out 10 to 12 small rounds of wax paper, line the bottom of each muffin cup, and spray with cooking spray. (This will prevent the topping from sticking to the bottom of the tin and will make for easier cleanup.) Place 1 teaspoon of topping in the bottom of each muffin cup, reserving the remaining topping for the glaze. Place the buns in the muffin cups, cut side up.

11. Bake until the buns are golden brown and firm to the touch, 28 to 30 minutes. Invert the buns onto a wire rack and let rest for 5 minutes with the pan still on top of the buns (this will help set the topping).

12. Place the buns on a serving plate and, using a pastry brush, glaze the sides and the tops of the buns with the reserved topping. Serve warm. This is easy to reheat in a 350°F oven for 10 minutes.

Tangerine Mimosa

SERVES 1

¾ cup Champagne or sparkling wine
¼ cup fresh tangerine juice
Mandarin oranges (fresh or from the can) or fresh clementines

In a Champagne flute, mix the Champagne with the juice. Serve with a mandarin orange section in the bottom of each flute.

PARK AVENUE HOLIDAY BRUNCH SOIRÉE

Around the holidays, food, family, and friends are always my first priority. For a holiday morning when family is in town, a more formal brunch, served buffet style, is a simple and beautiful way to feed a crowd. When I think of elegant, I think of Park Avenue in New York City, with stately apartments lining the block with their old-fashioned character.

Most of these dishes can be made ahead, so the morning of the party, just spend a few minutes setting up the buffet table with pretty trays. I like my buffets to look abundant, filled with baskets and trays of food. The party buffet can be set up in the kitchen, but if your kitchen is cramped, a good option is a six-foot fold-out table in the dining room. If you're expecting more than fifteen people, fill the dining room table full of food, and then people can eat and mingle in various rooms throughout the house—it's not as formal as everyone sitting down at one large table and makes for more relaxed entertaining, particularly on holidays, when people tend to eat all day long and at different times.

HOW TO SET UP A BUFFET TABLE

Holiday buffets should look beautiful. This is the time to pull out the good stuff—use the silver, the linen napkins, the nice trays. (Look for silver pieces at flea markets and keep your eye out for undiscovered treasures at thrift stores or garage sales; they usually just need a good polish.) It's all about making it special. You get dressed up for holidays, so dress up your table too.

Pull out all the serving pieces you may want to use ahead of time. Have your holiday menu in hand with a pad of yellow sticky notes and write down what food goes on which serving platter. Also, if you need to wash or shine the platters, use a different-colored sticky note to indicate that. This will help you organize and identify what needs to get done.

TABLE DECORATIONS

Think of the colors you associate with the particular holiday when choosing flowers and fruits to decorate the table. The decorations can be whimsical and fun: you could fill a big vase with live fish or set five bowls on the table, each with a floating flower such as an orchid, and an apple or a pear sitting upright between bowls. (At one party I catered, we used little Pyrex bowls in a pinch.) You'll get a very modern look, and your guests will find it très chic. Or place a big basket in the middle of the table and fill it with poinsettias, hydrangeas, mini pumpkins, or gourds, depending on the season. If you're a modernist, you might prefer tall, thin vases with a freshly cut branch or greens. Even weeds are pretty if you arrange them the right way.

Floral spray, which is a special type of paint used on things like flowers, plants, pottery, and wood, adds instant color, and it can be found at floral supply stores and art supply stores. I sometimes finish both flowers and centerpieces with Miracle-Gro Leaf Shine to give them a sheen. You can use an acrylic paint or, if you're working ahead, a high-gloss oil paint (which takes three or four days to dry) on items like flowerpots or even cardboard boxes. I gave one party a fun look by hand-painting all the clients' flowerpots bright yellow and filling them with blue and pink hydrangeas. It's an easy way to dress up a backyard or a porch.

To give an antique look to a pear, a pumpkin, or a flowerpot, spray it with some gold or silver floral spray and let it sit for an hour. Take a bristle brush or a nail brush and scrape some paint off, and it will instantly look aged. You can easily make terra-cotta pots look old by giving them a patina of moss: rub or paint them with plain yogurt, let them sit in the shade for a few days, and a nice green moss will form. I often spray my plants and leaves with Miracle-Gro Leaf Shine, a natural spray that gives leaves a glossy, bright green look. (Also keep green wire on hand to wire leaves or flowers.)

Lulu's Tip

Don't use large platters if you don't have that much food; think small and plentiful. All your platters should be piled high—it's more inviting, a feast for the eyes.

Place Cards

There are two different types of place cards: one for identifying dishes on a buffet and another for seating guests at the dinner table. Place cards, like name tags, aren't necessary but are a fun addition to a party. For the buffet, make place cards that identify each dish. Place cards help you avoid the constant barrage of questions about what each dish is. You can buy the cards or make them on your computer. Ceramic place cards can be found at most art stores and are easy to write on with a Sharpie pen, or you can hook name tags to

clothespins. Even a leaf can be used on the buffet; just write the name of the dish in gold pen. Small picture frames are another easy way to identify dishes. Another trick is to use paint chips. Go to your local hardware store, grab a handful of paint chips, cut off the name of the paint if visible, and tape them to toothpicks. You can write your guests' names or the name of the dish on them. Pretty stones can also make unique place settings: use smooth black stones and write the guests' names in gold pen or a pink paint pen, available at art supply stores.

For a kids' party, grab the paint chips for Disney paints; they have the Mickey Mouse logo on them, which is fun for the kids. (You can also punch a hole in the paint chips and use them as gift tags.) You might even have your kids (or nieces and nephews) make the place cards, either by hand or on a computer. My nieces Brittany, Kaleigh, and Quinnie love to do this. They are all very creative.

Polaroid photos make great place cards for a seated brunch, or if you don't have a Polaroid camera, use a digital camera and home photo printer. Snap a picture of the guests as they arrive and write their name on the photo with a silver or gold pen. Or use fruit: make a slit across the top of small apples, pears, clementines, lemons, or limes and stick a place card in the opening. During the winter holidays, secure a place card in a pinecone or even a wine cork (just cut a slit across the top).

Spiral Ham with Lulu's Mustard

This mustard is a good staple to keep in your fridge—it's good on just about anything. It's delicious with chicken and fish, and I love to dip pretzels in it.

SERVES 20

One 16- to 18-pound cooked spiral ham (see Sources)

½ cup dry mustard

½ teaspoon black pepper

¼ teaspoon white pepper

¼ teaspoon cayenne

1½ cups cider vinegar

1 teaspoon salt

2 cups sugar

4 tablespoons (½ stick) unsalted butter

2 whole eggs

2 egg yolks

① Preheat the oven to 350°F. Let the ham stand at room temperature for at least 30 minutes before baking.

② Make the mustard: In a medium saucepan over low heat, mix the dry mustard, black pepper, white pepper, and cayenne with ½ cup water and heat slightly. Do not inhale the mixture (it will clear your sinuses).

③ With the pan still over low heat, stir in the vinegar, salt, sugar, and butter.

④ In a separate bowl, beat the eggs and egg yolks together and whisk them into the mixture, stirring constantly until it thickens. If the mixture becomes lumpy, strain it through a mesh strainer. The mustard can be stored in the refrigerator in a sealed container for up to 2 weeks.

⑤ Brush the ham with half the mustard and bake for about 1 hour, or until the ham is heated through and the outside is caramelized and brown. Serve at room temperature with the remaining mustard.

Roasted Turkey

My father always made the turkey at our house. A few years ago, when he was visiting me in Los Angeles, a celebrity client called and asked me to prepare a full turkey dinner in the middle of September. Since I had never roasted a turkey, my dad happily agreed to roast the turkey for me and showed me his tricks. I took my dad with me when I dropped off the meal, which thrilled him, and I'll never forget how to roast a turkey.

SERVES 18 TO 20

One 18- to 20-pound turkey
½ pound (2 sticks) salted butter, softened
5 fresh rosemary sprigs, chopped, plus 5 whole sprigs
5 fresh thyme sprigs, chopped, plus 5 whole sprigs
20 garlic cloves, peeled
1 tablespoon plus 2 teaspoons salt

4 teaspoons white pepper
3 lemons, halved
2 oranges, halved
1 Granny Smith apple, quartered
1 onion, peeled and cut into quarters
1 quart turkey broth (I like Better Than Bouillon's turkey base because it's rich in flavor)

① Preheat the oven to 350°F.

② Rinse the turkey under cold running water. Dry the inside of the cavity and the outside skin with paper towels. Fit a large roasting pan with a V-rack lined with tinfoil and sprayed with cooking spray. Pierce the foil with a small knife several times. Place the turkey breast side up in the rack.

③ In a food processor, blend the butter, rosemary, thyme, and garlic with 1 tablespoon salt and 2 teaspoons pepper until smooth.

④ Loosen the skin from the breast meat and rub one-quarter of the herb butter onto each breast.

⑤ Rub the lemons and oranges all over the outside of the turkey and squeeze the juices onto the skin.

⑥ Season the cavity with 1 teaspoon each of the remaining salt and pepper and stuff with the lemons, oranges, apple, onion, and sprigs of rosemary and thyme.

⑦ Rub half the remaining herb butter on the skin of the turkey.

⑧ Flip the turkey over, breast side down, and rub the remaining herb butter all over the turkey. Season with the remaining teaspoon each of salt and pepper. Pour the turkey broth into the pan.

9. Roast the turkey for 3 hours, basting periodically.

10. Flip the bird breast side up and roast for 1 hour more.

11. Increase the heat to 400°F and roast for 1 hour more, or until the thickest part of the thigh registers 170°F to 175°F on a meat thermometer.

12. Remove from the oven and transfer to a cutting board or rimmed sheet pan. Cover loosely with foil and let stand for 20 to 30 minutes before carving.

13. Strain the juices from the pan and serve alongside the turkey.

Lulu's Baked Beans

My brother Byrne and I loved baked beans with a fried egg on top and fried tomatoes. Leftover beans were used to make bean sandwiches on toast.

SERVES 8 TO 10

Three 15-ounce cans Great Northern or navy beans
½ pound bacon, chopped
3 shallots, finely chopped
1 medium onion, finely chopped
2 tablespoons packed brown sugar
⅔ cup molasses

2 teaspoons dry mustard
1 tablespoon plus 1 teaspoon salt
½ teaspoon pepper
1 tablespoon Worcestershire sauce
1 tablespoon soy sauce
½ teaspoon hot red pepper flakes

1. Drain the beans in a colander and rinse them with cold water.

2. Place the bacon in a large saucepan over low heat and cook until crisp. Remove the bacon with a slotted spoon and drain on paper towels.

3. Add the shallots and onion to the pan and cook over low heat until softened, about 5 minutes.

4. Add the brown sugar, molasses, dry mustard, salt, pepper, Worcestershire, soy sauce, red pepper flakes, bacon, and 1 cup water. Stir in the beans and raise the heat to medium-high. Bring to a simmer and cook for 20 minutes, stirring constantly, until the mixture thickens slightly.

5. Serve hot or at room temperature. You can freeze any leftover beans.

Vegetable Herb Frittata

I learned about frittatas when I was working for the famous Sarah Leah Chase, author of the best Nantucket cookbooks. That summer I was a counter girl who eagerly took in everything that was going on in the store. I loved working for her; she was like an artsy Julia Child.

This is my own rendition of a frittata, inspired by the ones I used to sell at Que Sera Sarah. Three cheers for my dear friend Sarah Leah Chase!

SERVES 10 TO 12

1 large red onion, finely chopped

2 scallions, both white and green parts, thinly sliced

4 garlic cloves, minced

1 yellow squash, cut lengthwise into ¼-inch slices

1 zucchini, cut lengthwise into ¼-inch slices

1 red bell pepper, chopped

1 orange bell pepper, chopped

1 yellow bell pepper, chopped

2 cups stale sourdough French bread in small cubes

1 cup thinly sliced red potato

12 large eggs

½ cup heavy cream

1 teaspoon sugar

1 tablespoon Lawry's Seasoned Salt

2 teaspoons ground white pepper

8 ounces cream cheese, cut into small pieces

1½ cups grated Gruyère or Asiago cheese (or one 12-ounce bag grated four-cheese blend)

½ cup crumbled goat cheese

1 cup julienned raw spinach

2 tablespoons julienned fresh basil

2 tablespoons chopped fresh dill

2 tablespoons chopped fresh cilantro

½ teaspoon Tabasco sauce

① Preheat the oven to 350°F. Spray the bottom and sides of a 10-inch springform pan with nonstick spray.

② In a large bowl, combine all the vegetables, cubed bread, and potato slices.

③ In a medium bowl, whisk together the eggs, cream, sugar, seasoned salt, pepper, cheeses, spinach, herbs, and Tabasco.

④ Pour the egg mixture into the vegetable mixture and stir to combine.

⑤ Pour the mixture into the pan and place the pan on a tinfoil-covered baking sheet (this will keep the oven clean).

⑥ Bake for about 1 hour. Cover the top with foil and bake for 30 minutes more. When done, the frittata should puff up like a cake and be golden brown.

⑦ Let the frittata cool for a few minutes before slicing. The frittata can be served hot, at room temperature, or even cold.

Cheddar and Ham Biscuits

MAKES 12 BISCUITS

1¾ cups all-purpose flour
1 teaspoon cream of tartar
½ teaspoon baking soda
2 teaspoons sugar
1 teaspoon salt
½ teaspoon white pepper
4 tablespoons (½ stick) cold salted
  butter, diced

1 cup finely grated sharp Cheddar
  cheese
1⅓ cups finely diced ham
½ cup sliced scallion, both white and
  green parts
⅔ cup heavy cream
2 large eggs
1 tablespoon milk

1. Preheat the oven to 425°F. Lightly oil a baking sheet.

2. Sift the flour, cream of tartar, baking soda, sugar, salt, and pepper into the bowl of a food processor. Add the butter and pulse until the mixture forms coarse crumbs.

3. Place the mixture into a large bowl and, using a fork, stir in the cheese, ham, and scallion.

4. In a small bowl, beat the heavy cream with one of the eggs and add it to the flour mixture. Stir just until a rough, soft dough forms.

5. Turn the dough out onto a floured work surface and knead lightly until the dough clings together and is soft and puffy, about 1 minute.

6. Gently roll out the dough into rounds about ¾ inch thick. Dust a 2¼-inch round cookie cutter with flour and, using a quick, sharp motion, cut out biscuits as close together as possible. Gather the scraps of dough, knead briefly, roll out, and cut additional biscuits. Place the biscuits 1½ inches apart on the baking sheet.

7. To make the egg wash, whisk together the remaining egg and the milk. Lightly brush the tops of each biscuit with egg wash using a pastry brush.

8. Bake until the biscuits are golden brown, about 15 minutes. Serve hot or let cool to room temperature on a wire rack and serve with softened butter.

NOTE: The biscuits should be eaten within 3 days of baking and are best served warm.

Chocolate-Banana Bread

I've loved banana bread since I was a kid. One afternoon my nephew Mac Killian decided he wanted chocolate sauce over his piece of banana bread. I told him the next time we made it I would add chocolate chips instead, and that's where chocolate-banana bread started for the Powers/Killian clans. Whether it has chocolate in it or not, I still love eating a piece toasted with butter spread on top—delicious! You can serve it at room temperature for breakfast or warm with vanilla ice cream and whipped cream for dessert. The list of garnishes is endless, so be creative.

MAKES 1 LOAF

1 cup all-purpose flour

1 cup whole wheat flour

1½ teaspoons baking soda

1 teaspoon baking powder

1 teaspoon salt

1 cup pureed banana (about 2 ripe bananas)

½ cup packed brown sugar

½ cup granulated sugar

3 large eggs

8 tablespoons (1 stick) unsalted butter, quartered, at room temperature

½ cup buttermilk or yogurt

2 teaspoons vanilla extract

1½ cups chocolate chips

① Preheat the oven to 350°F. Butter and flour a 9 x 5-inch loaf pan.

② Combine the flours, baking soda, baking powder, and salt in a bowl and mix with a whisk.

③ Place the banana in the bowl of a food processor and puree. Add the sugars and eggs and process for 1 minute. Add the butter and process for 1 minute more. With the machine running, pour the buttermilk and vanilla through the feed tube. Add the flour mixture and chocolate chips and pulse 4 to 5 times, just until the batter is blended. (You can also prepare the batter by hand; just be sure to mash the bananas completely with a fork.)

④ Pour the batter into the loaf pan. (You can also use regular or mini muffin pans or 5 mini loaf pans.) Bake for 1 hour, or until the bread is brown and a knife or skewer inserted in the center comes out clean. (Bake the muffins for 20 to 25 minutes, mini loaves for 40 to 45 minutes.) Turn the bread onto a wire rack to cool. Baked and cooled banana bread can be frozen for up to 1 month in a freezer bag.

NOTE: Try using different flours for this cake. You could use 2 cups all-purpose flour instead of half white and half wheat. I've used rice flour and almond flour when baking for a gluten-intolerant friend.

Spicy English Breakfast Sausage Rolls

This recipe was inspired by my best friend Alison, who always made sausage rolls growing up in Australia.

MAKES 16 PIECES

1 tablespoon olive oil

1 onion, minced

1 pound turkey sausage, removed from casings

1 pound spicy pork sausage, removed from casings*

2 teaspoons ground allspice

1 tablespoon fennel seeds

2 tablespoons grade A or B maple syrup

3 ounces (6 tablespoons) cream cheese, at room temperature

One 17-ounce package puff pastry sheets (I use Pepperidge Farm), thawed

2 tablespoons Dijon mustard

① Preheat the oven to 400°F. Line a baking sheet with a Silpat baking mat or spray it with nonstick cooking spray.

② Heat the olive oil in a skillet over medium heat and sauté the onion until translucent, about 5 minutes.

③ Add the sausage meat, allspice, fennel seeds, and 1 tablespoon of the maple syrup and stir. Use a potato masher to break up the meat while it cooks. Sauté the meat mixture until the sausage is cooked through and any liquid has evaporated, about 5 minutes.

④ Add the cream cheese and mix until completely incorporated. Remove from the heat.

⑤ On a lightly floured work surface, roll out each of the two puff pastry sheets just until the seams disappear and the dough is rectangular in shape.

⑥ In a small bowl, combine the remaining 1 tablespoon maple syrup and the mustard. Using a pastry brush, brush half of the mixture onto the puff pastry.

⑦ Using a spatula, spread half the meat mixture evenly across each pastry piece, leaving a ½-inch border at either end of the shorter sides.

⑧ Starting from the shorter side of one piece of pastry, gently fold the dough over 3 times. Pinch the seams together and then roll the dough over so that the seam is on the bottom. Repeat with the second piece of pastry.

*If you can't find spicy pork sausage, use regular pork sausage plus 1 teaspoon hot red pepper flakes.

9. Cut across each sausage roll in 2-inch slices to create 8 pieces from each roll and brush with the remaining mustard mixture.

10. Lay the pastry pieces 2 to 3 inches apart on the baking sheet.

11. Bake for 20 to 25 minutes, or until golden brown and puffy.

12. Remove the puffs from the pan and place them on paper towels to drain any excess liquid. Serve hot.

Asparagus with Hollandaise Sauce

SERVES 6 TO 8

1 pound asparagus, trimmed
2 teaspoons olive oil
Salt and pepper to taste
1¼ cups Blender Hollandaise Sauce (recipe follows)

1. Preheat the oven to 400°F.

2. Spread the asparagus in a single layer on a jelly-roll pan. Sprinkle 1 tablespoon of water and the olive oil evenly over the top.

3. Bake for 10 minutes (5 minutes if the asparagus are pencil-thin), turning the asparagus once.

4. Season to taste with salt and pepper. Serve with hollandaise.

Blender Hollandaise Sauce

MAKES 1¼ CUPS

½ pound (2 sticks) unsalted butter
4 large egg yolks
2 tablespoons heavy cream
1 tablespoon freshly squeezed lemon
  juice

⅛ teaspoon salt
⅛ teaspoon white pepper
⅛ teaspoon Tabasco sauce

① Melt the butter in a small saucepan over low heat until very hot, but don't let it brown.

② Combine the egg yolks, heavy cream, lemon juice, salt, white pepper, and Tabasco in a blender. Turn the blender on low speed and blend.

③ With the blender on low speed, remove the cover and pour in the hot butter in a steady stream.

④ Use immediately, refrigerate, or freeze. To freeze, transfer the sauce to a freezer container, leaving ½ inch of space on top. Let cool, cover, and freeze. To reheat, heat the sauce in the top of a double boiler.

Lulu's Kir Royale

My clients love this festive and flirty drink, especially my client and design guru Kelly Wearstler. This is her staple party drink and she's wild about the ice cubes.

SERVES 1

1 tablespoon Chambord
6 ounces Champagne or sparkling wine, well chilled

Pour the Chambord into a Champagne flute and add the Champagne.

Lulu's Tip

It's easy to add a colorful sugar rim to a cocktail glass: simply moisten the rim of the Champagne flute with water and dip it into a bowl of superfine sugar. Buy colored sugar for a festive twist or make your own: place 1 cup superfine sugar on a piece of wax paper. Add a drop of food coloring and mix until the color is distributed evenly throughout the sugar. Continue adding food coloring, one drop at a time, until you're happy with the color. If the sugar comes out darker than you'd like, add more sugar. It keeps in an airtight container for up to 1 month.

Lulu's Tip

I like to garnish this drink with my own specialty ice cubes that I make using long ice cube trays from IKEA or Tupperware. I fill them with filtered water, add pomegranate seeds and sprigs of fresh thyme or rosemary, and freeze. I've also tried sliced kumquats and mint leaves. The cubes look beautiful floating in this drink or any other drink for that matter.

NOON

When I think of an afternoon party, I think lazy, hazy, and fun. An afternoon shindig can encompass a wide range of events—a summer barbecue, a child's birthday party, or a coast-inspired clambake. My clients seem more relaxed in the afternoon too. Whether you're hosting an all-ladies luncheon to celebrate an engagement or a baby-to-be, a cozy winter picnic, or a relaxing Sunday lunch, there are endless shortcuts for throwing a simple yet joyous party. It's easy to plan an afternoon get-together or celebration inside or outside, and if you don't have an outdoor area, like a backyard or a deck, just invite your friends to a local park.

Afternoon entertaining doesn't have to mean a formal, invite-only party; it can be impromptu, such as having a friend come over for a cocktail. My friend Leslie and I have done this many times around 4:00 P.M—drinking "juice," as I like to call an afternoon cocktail. (My father liked to say, "It has to be 5 o'clock somewhere!") These kinds of get-togethers take the edge off for me and give me a break from thinking about my work and just life in general. Life should be lived, so why not have a little "sneaky"? (A "sneaky" is a little drink in the afternoon, a term I learned from my dear ol' father.)

Of course, special drinks aren't just for adults. My mother would make the kids a special drink at her parties, such as grape juice, ginger ale, and Shirley Temples, which we were allowed to drink on Sundays after church or on a special occasion. (To this day, for most of my friends' kids, Shirley Temples are still a treat, especially if they're served with extra cherries.)

Because most of my family lives on the East Coast, I've started a Sunday tradition with my friends here in Los Angeles. Every Sunday Stevie and I go to our friends Kimm and Al Uzielli's house for lunch. Kimm is always trying out new recipes, and our friend Leslie usually brings ice cream to go along with whatever our friends Boris and Mona bring for dessert. Stevie and I always bring potato chips, dip, and the ingredients for a new cocktail. We try a different concoction every week. Making your own traditions and creating your own celebrations is a key component in entertaining. Where there is laughter there is love, and when you entertain, this dynamic should always come through.

LADIES WHO LUNCH

There's something about getting dressed up and spending the afternoon chatting that is so civilized. Most of the lunches I've attended are for charity, but the parties I've catered include birthdays, baby and bridal showers, and welcome lunches. The recipes here are inspired by the lunches I've thrown or attended over the years, with delicious but dainty recipes that no one can refuse.

I cater many product launches that demand formal lunches where elegance reigns, and the food needs to be clean and light. The guests always seem to be watching their figures at these lunches (well, at least in public). But my favorite ladies' lunch takes place at my own house, with four of my friends who like to dress up, eat up, and drink up. Even though a ladies' lunch might sound like a formal event, it can also mean having a couple of friends over for an afternoon of chatting and enjoying one another's company over a nice chicken salad.

Dressing up the table is a part of a more formal lunch, but it doesn't take a lot of time. Whether the table decoration is fruit or flowers, it should be low on the table, so it's easier to gossip while you eat! At these lunches the table is at least as important as the food. It's all about look, style, and elegance.

DÉCOR

For a more elegant ladies' lunch, use your china (or borrow it if you have to) or mix and match your best pieces. Do the same with the water and cocktail glasses. It's fun to use place cards for a luncheon; see page 66 for ideas.

Depending on the season, you can decorate the table with a variety of flowers or seasonal items: branches of kumquats, brightly colored fall leaves—whatever is available.

Just a single tulip in a vase can add elegance to a table. In the fall, apples (three separate bowls of different varieties of apples), dried corn husks, pumpkins, pomegranates, colorful autumn leaves, whole nuts (don't forget the nutcracker), crab apple branches, and fresh cranberries all make festive centerpieces.

In the winter, think of holly, ivy, pinecones, poinsettias, Christmas ornaments, mini nutcrackers, evergreen branches, and winter white. I love to cover a whole table in silver tinsel and set the plates on top of it. Miniature trees, such as rosemary trees, look beautiful and scent the room, as do paperwhites. Wintry touches such as cinnamon sticks tied with a green ribbon or spray-painted pinecones make any room look festive. A centerpiece consisting of ornaments in a pretty crystal or glass bowl is another easy wintertime trick. You can spray-paint leftover mini pumpkins in gold or silver. I am big on gold or silver spray-painting—from terra-cotta pots to match my décor to pinecones, fruit, and things like acorns that I find on the ground when I'm out walking.

Spring brings fresh blossoms and flowers arranged in clear glass vases; whole cut branches of spring blossoms are even more dramatic, while small glasses of tulips are easy and eye-catching.

I've even used empty Tiffany gift boxes as centerpieces: I filled them with floral foam and arranged flowers spilling over the edges. When I threw a "Breakfast at Tiffany's" party for a celebrity client, I borrowed Tiffany's gift boxes from my girlfriends, filled them with flowers and small bonsai trees with moss, and arranged them around the house. The bright blue boxes looked so festive.

Edible place settings are great for summer: big bowls of strawberries, blueberries, or cherries are simple and elegant. Seashells also look pretty placed in clear glass vases, and hydrangeas are one of summer's prettiest flowers. My favorite table decorations are long, low wooden bread trays of flowers, candy, crab apples, key limes, clementines, or even crackers placed down the table. These are great in any season; just add seasonal touches like sprigs of pine or evergreen in winter.

Apple and Root Vegetable Soup

I teach this recipe in my cooking classes. It's nutritious and easy to make, and everyone seems to really enjoy it.

MAKES 10 CUPS; SERVES 8 TO 10

8 tablespoons (1 stick) salted butter

2 cups coarsely chopped onion

2 cups peeled, cored, and coarsely chopped Granny Smith apple

2 cups peeled and coarsely chopped turnip

2 cups peeled and coarsely chopped butternut squash

2 cups coarsely chopped carrot

2 cups peeled and coarsely chopped sweet potato

10 cups salted chicken stock

1 teaspoon kosher salt, plus salt to taste

½ cup grade A or B maple syrup

Cayenne to taste

① Melt the butter in a large stockpot over moderately high heat.

② Add the onion and sauté until translucent, about 5 minutes. Add the apple, turnip, squash, carrot, sweet potato, stock, and 1 teaspoon salt.

③ Cook, stirring occasionally, for 30 to 35 minutes, or until the vegetables are tender.

④ Use a hand blender to puree the soup in the pot. (If you don't have a hand blender, pour the soup into a food processor and puree in batches.)

⑤ Transfer the pureed soup back to the pot and add the maple syrup and cayenne. Season to taste, bring the soup to a simmer, and serve.

JUST AN IDEA: For a heartier soup, add shredded roast chicken along with 1 cup heavy cream. Alternatively, add a cubed uncooked chicken breast along with the vegetables.

Asparagus with Prosciutto and Boursin

This old family recipe was a staple appetizer in my mom's catering business. It's different and easy to make.

SERVES 8 TO 10

1 pound Boursin cheese (Alouette or any soft garlic cheese can be substituted)
1 pound prosciutto, thinly sliced (see Note)
1 pound asparagus

① Preheat the oven to 450°F.

② Spread the Boursin cheese on the prosciutto slices and wrap them around the asparagus spears.

③ Lay the asparagus on a baking sheet and bake for 4 minutes. Cover and bake for 4 more minutes, or until the asparagus is tender, slightly brown, and almost crispy.

NOTE: You can also make this with smoked salmon. Bake the asparagus for 8 minutes at 400°F and then let it cool. Spread the smoked salmon slices with Boursin and wrap them around the asparagus spears.

Baguette Slices with Brie and Pear

This appetizer is *très Français*. It's best when the Brie is ripe and left at room temperature for at least 2 hours. Put a dribble of honey on it with a crack of pepper . . . *délicieux*.

SERVES 6 TO 8

16 thin slices French baguette
1 pound Brie
1 perfectly ripe pear, cored and thinly sliced
¼ cup honey
Salt and freshly ground black pepper

Lay the bread slices on a tray or baking sheet. Spread each slice with a spoonful of Brie, a slice of pear, and a dollop of honey. Sprinkle salt and pepper and serve.

Citrus-Glazed Salmon

I love salmon: sushi, carpaccio, baked, broiled, grilled—just about every which way. Not everybody likes fish, but I knew this was a hit when my nephew Andrew, who doesn't usually eat fish, asked me for seconds. It's good hot or at room temperature, perfect for lunch or dinner. You can use a whole side of salmon for a large party or a buffet.

SERVES 4

FOR THE SALMON

4 teaspoons white vinegar

Four 4-ounce salmon fillets
  (see headnote)

FOR THE MARINADE

2 tablespoons olive oil

3 tablespoons freshly squeezed lemon
  juice

3 tablespoons freshly squeezed lime
  juice

1 teaspoon Tabasco sauce

¼ cup grade A or B maple syrup

½ cup soy sauce

2 garlic cloves, crushed

1½ teaspoons salt

¼ teaspoon pepper

1 teaspoon grated fresh ginger
  (optional)

FOR THE GLAZE

¼ cup honey

1½ teaspoons soy sauce

1 garlic clove, crushed

1 tablespoon lime zest

1 teaspoon salt

½ teaspoon freshly ground black
  pepper

1 teaspoon grated fresh ginger
  (optional)

Salt and pepper to taste

① Pour a teaspoon of the white vinegar over each salmon fillet and rinse under very cold water to eliminate any fishy smell. (Soaking fish in milk will also take away the fishy smell.) Pat dry with paper towels and arrange the fillets in a shallow baking dish to marinate.

② To make the marinade, mix together all the ingredients and pour over the salmon. Let sit for at least 1 hour or refrigerate for up to 24 hours.

③ Remove the salmon from the refrigerator at least 30 minutes before cooking. Turn on the broiler. Line a sheet pan with aluminum foil and spray the foil with nonstick cooking spray. (This will make cleanup much easier.)

④ To make the glaze, mix together all the ingredients.

⑤ Place the salmon on the sheet pan and season lightly with salt and pepper. Brush the glaze liberally on the salmon and broil for 5 to 7 minutes, or until the top has caramelized. Serve immediately.

Escarole and Mesclun Salad
with Edamame, Mint, and Pecorino

SERVES 8 TO 10

2 cups (9 ounces) frozen shelled
  edamame

VINAIGRETTE
½ cup Champagne vinegar
2 small shallots, finely minced
1 teaspoon sugar
¼ cup coarsely chopped fresh parsley
1 cup extra virgin olive oil
Salt and pepper to taste

1½ pounds escarole, cut crosswise into
  very thin strips
1 pound mesclun greens
1 cup julienned fresh mint
1 cup finely grated Pecorino cheese
1 tablespoon plus 1 teaspoon lemon zest

① Bring a 3-quart pot of salted water to a boil and cook the edamame for 5
   minutes. Drain the edamame in a colander and rinse under cold running
   water to stop the cooking. Drain the edamame again and pat dry.

② To make the vinaigrette, combine the vinegar, shallots, sugar, parsley,
   and olive oil in a blender and blend until smooth. Season to taste with
   salt and pepper.

③ Toss the edamame, escarole, mesclun greens, and mint together in a
   large bowl. Add the Pecorino, drizzle the salad with the vinaigrette, and
   toss again. Garnish with the lemon zest.

Banana Zabaglione with Fresh Berries and Rosemary Shortbread Cookies

My husband has a definite sweet tooth, and this is one of his favorite desserts. He likes the zabaglione over strawberries with a cookie and a cup of fresh mint tea. I use any berries I have on hand, especially blackberries when they're in season. It's great because you can make it ahead of time. You can give a nice-size portion or serve it in shot glasses with berries on top and a demitasse spoon.

MAKES ABOUT 3 CUPS; SERVES 8

8 large egg yolks
½ cup plus 1 tablespoon sugar
¾ cup banana liqueur
1½ cups heavy cream

2 cups fresh berries
Rosemary Shortbread cookies
  (recipe follows)

1. Combine the egg yolks, the ½ cup sugar, and the liqueur in the top of a double boiler or in a stainless-steel bowl above a saucepan of simmering water. (Make sure the bottom of the bowl does not touch the water.)

2. Whisk the custard mixture constantly for 8 to 10 minutes, or until it is light, creamy, and pale yellow. If you're serving the custard as a sauce, cook until slightly thickened. (Increasing the cooking time will thicken the custard to a mousselike texture.)

3. When it reaches the desired consistency, remove the sauce from the heat and continue whisking for a minute or two to prevent the custard from sticking.

4. Cool the zabaglione by placing the bowl in an ice bath (a larger bowl of ice and water).

5. In a mixer or food processor, beat the cream with the remaining 1 tablespoon sugar until it holds soft peaks. Fold the cream into the zabaglione, under the berries, with the shortbread on the side, and serve immediately or let it cool and refrigerate for up to 3 days.

Rosemary Shortbread Cookies

These are good with coffee, tea, or a warm cup of milk with a touch of honey.

MAKES 24

¾ pound (3 sticks) salted butter, at room temperature

⅔ cup sugar

2¾ cups all-purpose flour

¼ teaspoon salt

2 tablespoons chopped fresh rosemary

① Preheat the oven to 350°F.

② Cream the butter and sugar together in a mixing bowl or food processor until light and fluffy. Add the flour, salt, and rosemary. Cover and refrigerate for 1 hour.

③ On a lightly floured surface, roll the dough to a ¼-inch thickness. Using a cookie cutter, cut out cookies and arrange 1 inch apart on a sheet pan lined with Silpat or parchment paper. The scraps can be rolled out one more time to make additional cookies.

④ Bake for 8 to 10 minutes, or until the shortbread is light golden. Cool on a wire rack until ready to serve.

⑤ The cookies can be stored in an airtight container for up to 2 weeks. You can also freeze them, wrapped in plastic wrap in a Ziploc bag, for up to 1 month.

CHILD'S PLAY: A BIRTHDAY PARTY

Whatever happened to balloons, party hats, cake, and a simple game of pin the tail on the donkey? When I was little, my birthday parties were just a bunch of kids and my mom's famous sheet cake—a far cry from today's elaborate affairs.

You don't have to hire a caterer and a party planner to throw a birthday party for your child; you can do it yourself. It just takes a little planning, a little imagination, and a lot of patience! Ask your kids how they envision their party; all kids have ideas. The easiest trick? I always put out jars of candy, cookies, and fudge so everyone can help themselves to something sweet. This makes everyone smile. While some parents say giving sugar to kids is like giving them crack, I don't think you can have a kids' party without a healthy dose of candy. When my goddaughter Jazzie turned three, I asked her what kind of party she wanted. She replied, with hands flying in the air and her feet trying to tap dance, "A candy party!" She wanted two things at the party: candy and little hot dogs. I followed her instructions, and she was up until 3:00 A.M. from all the sugar while her mom passed out on the couch. In Jazzie's eyes, the party was a great success.

Another successful kids' party I threw recently was for my godson Jack Vein. All he wanted was animals; yellow, blue, and red cupcakes; doughnuts; and a jumpy house (an inflatable house the kids jump in). I bought animal balloons as well as yellow, blue, green, and red balloons and threw in some metallic silver balloons for a little pizzazz. I rented low kids' tables with red, blue, and white plastic kids' chairs and used bright yellow tablecloths. I got these great green frog watering cans filled with bright red gerbera daisies to weigh down the tables. I also found plastic ladybug bouncing balls and yellow balls with red polka dots and used tape to secure them to the table. At each kid's place setting was a box of animal crackers, and my crew and I tied balloons to each chair. It really looked like a fun celebration.

When planning the food, make sure you include the adults in your head count, because they'll definitely eat. I like to serve cocktails to calm the adults' nerves (the kids get juice boxes).

Check out the dollar stores or stores like Target for touches that will make any kids' party more fun. Get creative with the decorations and make up your own party games. If you're throwing a party indoors, the most important element is colored balloons, which signal "party" to kids.

Find balloons in all shapes and make sure the ribbons on the balloons are long enough that kids can grab them. Hang colorful streamers from the ceiling to add even more color.

Remember, don't make yourself crazy. The only important thing is to give kids what they want: cake, candy, and a goody bag (see "Party Favors," page 98). My sister's most successful kids' party was a sports party for her eleven-year-old son, Tucker, who is a sports fanatic. It started with touch football in the backyard, followed by lunch at a local sports-themed restaurant that was filled with televisions. She topped it off with an ice-cream cake, and the kids were ecstatic.

FUN PARTY TOUCHES

Decorating a space for a kids' party is limited only by your imagination—anything goes! A kids' party should be all about color. If it isn't colorful or doesn't seem fun, don't do it.

I've used kids' rubber Wellington boots as centerpieces and filled them with licorice and lollipops or with flowers. (You can find them at most children's shoe stores.) To decorate the ceiling, hang decorative items such as clouds or plastic or foam letters using string or brown twine. If your child loves animals, use stuffed animals to decorate the party space.

Think of a fun project or activity that will keep kids busy during the party. Art projects, such as making drums from coffee cans or stringing necklaces, give the kids something to take home with them. For younger kids, substitute uncooked macaroni shells for the beads and have them paint their "bracelets" with nontoxic paint. If the kids are older, however, forget about the tchotchkes and just go for the candy; the parents will thank you for not adding more stuff to their already full house! Another fun activity, depending on the child's age, is tying a piñata to a tree and letting kids take a crack at it. You can also fill the piñata with bags of cookies, pretzels, Goldfish, dried fruit, animal crackers, or small, inexpensive toys. Games like potato-sack races, musical chairs, Simon Says, and bobbing for apples are just good old-fashioned fun.

Finally, make the food fun! Use animal-shaped ice cube trays as Jell-O molds and serve the Jell-O on a colorful platter.

Party Favors

Every kid these days expects to go home with a goody bag or box. I love the circus cookies that come in a box—they make great party favors. I also make bags of candy tied with ribbon, but you could make cookies and put them in colored bags instead. Look in unexpected stores for party favor ideas: the ninety-nine-cent or dollar store and even the drugstore often carry inexpensive kids' toys that are perfect for giveaways. Mini chalkboards are a great favor. Just buy small, cheap wood-framed canvases at your local art store, spray them with chalkboard paint (available at most hardware stores), and wrap them with chalk and a ribbon. It's a great gift for boys and girls of all ages.

A personalized CD of your child's favorite songs is another great favor, and you can easily make CD labels with a computer. (This is great for kids ages seven and up.) Many parents try to tie the party favor to the theme of the party. My friend Alison gave Blockbuster gift cards as favors at her daughter's drive-in-movie-themed birthday.

My clients almost always splurge on favors. One woman handed out a board game to each child, and another client gave bags of jelly beans attached to plastic animals. You might even transform the candy jars into a pretend candy store; hand out cute plastic bags and let kids fill their own bags from the jars. Don't have glass candy jars? Go to your local hardware store and buy clean, empty paint cans. Fill each can with one type of candy. Write the name of the candy on the can with a paint pen or stick a clean, wooden paint stirrer in each bucket and write the name of the candy on the stirrer.

Of course, I personally think the best gifts are books. Get a whole bunch of age-appropriate books and put ribbons around them—you can't go wrong.

Mini Banana–Peanut Butter Sandwiches

Does it get better than this? These are good any time of day, even for dessert with a dollop of whipped cream.

SERVES 20

1 loaf potato bread, sliced
1 jar almond or peanut butter
1 bunch of ripe bananas, thinly sliced
4 tablespoons (½ stick) salted butter

① Lay the slices of bread on a cookie sheet, spreading half the bread slices with almond butter and then layering banana slices on top. Add the remaining bread slices on top to form sandwiches.

② Melt 2 tablespoons of the butter in a large sauté pan over medium heat. Add 4 or 5 sandwiches to the sauté pan at a time and cook for 2 minutes per side, or until golden brown.

③ Add 2 tablespoons of butter to the pan before cooking the next batch and repeat with the remaining sandwiches.

④ Let the sandwiches cool, cut off the crusts, and cut into quarters (for about 40 pieces). Serve warm.

Lulu's Puff Pastry Turkey Sliders

These are great for kids as well as adults, and they're perfect to serve with salad for lunch or dinner.

MAKES 32 SLIDERS

FOR THE TURKEY SLIDERS
1 pound ground turkey
1 egg (any size)
1½ cups Pepperidge Farm seasoned
  bread crumbs
¼ cup diced onion
¼ cup chopped fresh cilantro
¾ cup cranberry sauce
1 tablespoon freshly squeezed
  lime juice
1 tablespoon minced garlic
1 tablespoon ground cumin
¼ teaspoon cayenne
2 teaspoons salt
Two 17-ounce packages Pepperidge
  Farm puff pastry sheets, thawed

FOR THE CURRY AÏOLI
½ cup mayonnaise
1 teaspoon curry powder
½ teaspoon smoked paprika
3 garlic cloves, crushed
1 tablespoon freshly squeezed
  lime juice
Zest of 1 lime
2 scallions, both white and green parts,
  minced
1 tablespoon grade A or B maple syrup
Salt and pepper to taste

32 arugula leaves

① Preheat the oven to 375°F. Line two large baking sheets with Silpat baking mats.

② In a large bowl, mix the ground turkey, egg, bread crumbs, onion, cilantro, cranberry sauce, lime juice, garlic, cumin, cayenne, and salt just until the ingredients are incorporated.

③ Form the mixture into 2-inch patties and place the patties 1 inch apart on each baking sheet.

④ Unroll the puff pastry on a clean surface. Use the cookie cutter to cut out 2-inch circles. Place the pastry circles 1 inch apart to fill each baking sheet. (You want to end up with one circle per patty.) Bake each sheet for 20 to 25 minutes, or until the pastry is puffed and golden brown.

⑤ While the sliders and the pastry are baking, whisk together the aïoli ingredients in a small mixing bowl.

6. To assemble the sliders, place one turkey patty on a pastry circle. Pull each circle apart gently so you are left with the top and the bottom. Top with an arugula leaf and a dollop of aïoli and then top with another pastry circle. Repeat with the remaining patties and pastry circles.

NOTE: You can mix the burger ingredients, make the patties, and cut out the pastry circles ahead of time. Just put the burgers and puff pastry circles on a baking sheet lined with a Silpat baking mat, cover with plastic wrap, and freeze until ready to use. Thaw the patties and pastry circles for 20 minutes and then bake each sheet for 20 to 25 minutes, until the pastry is puffed and golden brown.

Mini Hot Dogs

My goddaughter Jazzie loves to come to my house to make these little dogs. They're always a hit, even at the fanciest parties. I usually serve them with my homemade mustard (page 67). Most little kids like them with ketchup, though, so when I'm serving both kids and adults I put out bowls of each.

SERVES 20

2 packages (12 ounces) Hebrew National cocktail franks or Aidell's mini chicken and apple sausages (or any brand mini–hot dog or sausage)
2 packages (17.3 ounces) refrigerated crescent roll dough or Pepperidge Farm puff pastry

1. Preheat the oven to 400°F.

2. Wrap each hot dog or sausage in a piece of crescent roll dough just until the edges meet. The ends of each hotdog will stick out. Lay on a greased baking sheet.

3. Bake for 15 to 20 minutes, until the dough is golden brown.

NOTE: The hot dogs can be made up to one month ahead and frozen. It's easiest to cook them halfway and then freeze them. Wrap the half-cooked hot dogs in the dough and then wrap tightly in plastic wrap. Heat still frozen in a 400°F oven for 15 minutes.

Mini Cheese Quesadillas

These are easy and simple. At one party a child asked me for some ranch dressing and Tabasco. I happened to have some, and this cute little boy mixed the Tabasco with the dressing and dipped the quesadilla in it.

SERVES 20

1 package flour tortillas
4 cups shredded Monterey Jack cheese or *queso fresco* (Mexican fresh cheese)
2 tablespoons canola or neutral-flavored cooking oil
Salsa, guacamole, or sour cream

① Using a 4-inch round cookie cutter, cut rounds out of the tortillas.

② Cover half the rounds with a heaping tablespoon of cheese and fold each round over to create little half-moons.

③ Heat 1 tablespoon of the oil in a sauté pan over medium heat and cook the quesadillas until the cheese is melted, about 3 minutes per side. Repeat with the remaining quesadillas, adding the second tablespoon of oil as needed.

④ Serve hot with salsa, guacamole, or sour cream.

Carrots and Celery with Pink Dip

This dip brings back many fond childhood memories. We always enjoyed it at birthday parties with carrots and celery and Fritos corn chips.

MAKES 2 CUPS; SERVES 10

FOR THE DIP
Half 8-ounce package cream cheese, at room temperature
½ cup sour cream
½ cup bottled French dressing
1 garlic clove, pressed
½ teaspoon Tabasco sauce
1 tablespoon freshly squeezed lemon juice

½ teaspoon salt
½ teaspoon ground white pepper

FOR SERVING
1 bag baby carrots
1 bunch of celery, cut into small sticks

In a large bowl, mix together all the dip ingredients until well blended. Serve with the carrots and celery sticks. The dip can be made up to 2 days ahead and refrigerated. Bring to room temperature before serving.

Cinnamon Bites

This recipe was passed along to me by my sister Sue, whose kids are all obsessed with these little cinnamon bites. They're great with a cup of coffee or a cold glass of milk, and they'd be just as delicious served with ice cream for a tasty dessert.

MAKES 48 MINI BITES

FOR THE MUFFINS

1 large egg
½ cup milk
8 tablespoons (1 stick) salted butter, melted
1¾ cups all-purpose flour
¾ cup plus 2 tablespoons sugar
1 teaspoon ground cinnamon
2 teaspoons baking powder
¼ teaspoon salt

FOR THE TOPPING

8 tablespoons (1 stick) unsalted butter
2½ teaspoons vanilla extract
1½ teaspoons ground cinnamon
1 cup sugar

① Preheat the oven to 400°F. Spray 4 mini muffin pans with baking spray or canola spray.

② In the bowl of a food processor or in a mixer, combine the egg, milk, and melted butter until well blended. Add the flour, sugar, cinnamon, baking powder, and salt. Pulse in the food processor or mix with an electric mixer until incorporated.

③ Fill each cup in the muffin pan a little over half full. Bake for 10 to 12 minutes, or until golden brown.

④ To make the topping, melt the butter with the vanilla in a small skillet over low heat. In a small bowl, stir together the cinnamon and sugar.

⑤ When the muffins are ready, take them out of the pan immediately and have your cooling racks ready. (You may need to use a knife around the edges if they stick.)

⑥ Roll the muffins in the melted butter and then in the cinnamon-sugar mixture.

⑦ Transfer the muffins to cooling racks until the topping is set.

NOTE: You can freeze the muffins in a sealed storage container for up to 1 month (if you use a Ziploc bag, they will be squished).

Pudding Pops

Every kid in America loves these pops. They're easy to make in bulk and store in the freezer.

MAKES 24

One 5-ounce package chocolate pudding mix
One 5-ounce package vanilla pudding mix
Dixie cups or Popsicle molds
Wooden Popsicle sticks

1. Make the pudding according to the instructions on the pudding packages.

2. Meanwhile, lightly spray each Dixie cup or Popsicle mold with nonstick baking spray.

3. Fill each cup halfway with either vanilla or chocolate pudding.

4. Place the molds on a sheet pan and put them into the freezer for 1 hour.

5. Remove the molds from the freezer and pour in the second layer of either vanilla or chocolate pudding.

6. Place a Popsicle stick into the middle of each one and freeze for another hour.

7. When you're ready to serve the pudding pops, remove them from the freezer and let them sit for 5 minutes. Peel off the Dixie cups or remove them from the molds and serve.

NOTE: If you want to make a swirl pop, put a layer of vanilla and a layer of chocolate in each mold and swirl the mixture with a toothpick.

THE CELEBRATORY SHOWER

It seems there's a shower every week, whether it's celebrating a wedding or a baby, and it's truly the perfect way to mark the occasion. A mix of appetizers and light bites is perfect for chatting and eating the afternoon away. A tea party–themed shower is an easy way to create a simple celebration for a baby-to-be or an upcoming wedding. Tea parties are divine and so versatile, and almost everything can be made ahead, so the day of the party you just have to boil water and set out the trays.

While sandwiches and appetizers always make the table look fabulous, salads are perfect for a shower; you can prep them ahead and toss them at the last minute or serve the dressing on the side. And salads don't mean just crisp greens—you can make fabulous salads using lentils, rice, and vegetables and serve them hot or cold. Even the most complicated salad is easy to put out for guests: place the ingredients in separate bowls and let guests assemble their salad on their own plate. Certain salads are better left undressed. When guests add their own dressing, they can eat when they want, and you don't have to worry about soggy salads.

Drinks are an essential element of any shower. Coffee and tea are a must, but I like to go beyond the standard selections. I always have a nonalcoholic party drink for any pregnant women, as well as a Champagne cocktail or wine. My other standbys are the Arnold Palmer (half iced tea, half lemonade) and strawberry lemonade. If you're expecting kids, have hot chocolate ready. Even if you're hosting a tea party, don't think that guests won't want a glass of something stronger (it's still a tea party without the tea). At one tea I catered, the women indulged in more wine and Champagne than the fresh mint tea we were serving. It was a group of old friends who had gathered to honor a bride-to-be, and they spent the afternoon talking, snacking, and drinking. Now that's a good time! And in case the party moves into the evening and guests linger, keep some extra bottles of white wine and Champagne on hand.

DÉCOR

Decorating your space for a shower is easy. For a bridal shower, buy yards of white tulle at a fabric store and use it wherever you like: drape it on the buffet table, the gift table, or around the cake. (At one shower I catered, I draped white tulle around a dark chocolate cake, and it looked beautiful.) For a baby shower, use pink, blue, green, or yellow tulle with rose petals or plastic baby rattles. Small wooden baby blocks are fun as well. I also like to decorate the tulle. For one shower I sewed baby socks onto the fabric and then arranged it on the table, but you could safety-pin them to save time. You might also take a piece of string and run it across the room and use clothespins to hang baby socks, hats, and shirts that are then given as gifts to the mother-to-be.

When you're setting the table for a tea party, use a variety of different teapots, mixing porcelain and silver if you have both. It's fun to have a teapot for each person if you can, and I like to serve the tea in little demitasse cups. If you don't have teacups, put out a matching set of mugs or borrow a set from a friend. I always put out a bowl of almonds for people to snack on.

Tea parties require colorful, festive flowers on the table. Find the brightest flowers of the season; my favorite are orange tulips.

If you use a colorful tablecloth, just go with flowers in one color. Even white carnations can look beautiful in a simple mirrored or glass vase.

Use cake stands or three-tiered serving stands to serve the food, as well as pretty platters. And remember that you can always rent items like teapots and tea sets (see page 5 for more on party rentals).

PARTY FAVORS

I personally don't believe in favors for weddings, showers, or adult birthday parties. You're coming to celebrate someone else, so why do you need to leave with a gift? As a host, you shouldn't feel that you have to give something back to your guests. If you feel the need to do something, instead of spending money on favors, take the money and donate it to a children's charity. Leave a little note at each guest's place setting to let them know about it.

My cousin Paula chose this approach and expanded the concept for her own wedding. At each place setting, she left a letterpress card telling guests that, in lieu of favors, she had made a donation to a charity that was close to her heart. Her close friend's two-year-old son was battling cancer at the time, and she made a donation in his honor. On the card, she recognized cancer survivors not only in the family but among her friends as well. Everyone was touched, and, frankly, who wouldn't want to give up a silly gift to help those in need? It still brings tears to my eyes.

SHOWER GAMES

Everyone is usually too busy chatting and eating at a party to play games, but at certain parties people expect some sort of game. My favorite bridal shower game is fairly simple: Split the guests into two or three teams. Using a guest as a dressmaker's dummy, each team has to make a dress out of toilet paper, and the best dress wins. You could also make up a funny multiple-choice quiz about the bride and have guests fill it out; the guest with the most correct answers gets a prize.

At one baby shower I attended, everyone put in $20 ahead of time to bet on when the child would be born. We knew the baby was due on February 18, and I had the closest guess—the baby was born on the father's birthday, February 16. The betting pool had a whopping $120 in it, which I used to open up baby Liam's first bank account.

If the mom-to-be hasn't named the baby yet, have the guests suggest a few names on a piece of paper and throw them into a bowl. Read them out loud; you'd be surprised at what people come up with! You could also have guests place first-name ideas in one bowl and middle-name ideas in a second bowl and mix and match.

Tea Primer

Whether you like strong black tea, earthy green tea, or soothing herbal tea, tea is all the rage these days, available in virtually every flavor and variety you can think of. I love to go to Le Palais des Thés, a specialty tea store in Beverly Hills, and browse through the rows and rows of tea; it's amazing to see the different leaves and smell the different aromas. Plus, they have beautiful displays that always give me ideas (see Sources).

One of my favorite teas is Jasmine Pearl, which opens up into beautiful flowers and gives off a wonderful fragrance. I like to use big Bolla wineglasses to serve the tea; guests love the surprise of the tea unfolding before their eyes. Clear glass teapots are another way to see the beautiful tea leaves bloom. There are many types of flowering teas, and they look as spectacular as they taste.

It's easy enough to tear open a tea bag, but if you want to brew loose tea, just remember these tips:

* Boil fresh water (I like to use filtered water) in a kettle on the stove or use an electric kettle. If you're serving green tea, don't bring the water to a full boil—boiling water cooks the delicate green tea leaves and destroys their flavor.

* Use 1 tablespoon loose tea per cup of tea.

* Steep tea for 2 to 3 minutes, strain, and pour.

If you're using tea bags instead of loose tea, look for tea in "silk" pouches rather than paper tea bags. Many paper tea bags contain tea dust, while the pouches contain loose tea leaves, which are more flavorful. (See Sources.) If you use tea bags containing tea dust, you won't need to steep your tea for as long.

Lulu's Tip

Remember to have coffee on hand for those who don't like tea! And in the event that the tea party moves into the evening as guests linger, keep some extra bottles of chilled white wine and Champagne on hand.

Roast Beef, Cranberry, and Spinach Rolls with Horseradish Aïoli

I've been making these wraps since the fifth grade.

MAKES ABOUT 50 PIECES

½ cup mayonnaise

Half 8-ounce package cream cheese, softened

1 teaspoon white pepper

1 teaspoon salt

1 teaspoon sugar

1 tablespoon prepared horseradish

1 package 10-inch flour tortillas (about 10 tortillas)

1½ pounds thinly sliced roast beef

1 cup dried cranberries

One 12-ounce bag baby spinach

1. To make the aïoli, in a large bowl cream together the mayonnaise, cream cheese, pepper, salt, sugar, and horseradish.

2. To assemble the sandwiches, using a spatula, apply a thin layer of aïoli on one side of each tortilla, leaving a ½-inch border around the edge.

3. Lay a slice of roast beef on top of each tortilla and sprinkle a tablespoon or so of cranberries and a layer of spinach evenly across the beef. Starting from one end, roll the wraps tightly.

4. Slice each wrap into 1½-inch rolls and serve them cut side up.

Open-Faced Cucumber and Tomato Tea Sandwiches

MAKES ABOUT 40 SANDWICHES

½ loaf thinly sliced potato bread
1 cup Boursin cheese, store-bought or
   homemade (page 41)
1 hothouse cucumber, thinly sliced into
   about 40 slices
8 plum tomatoes, each cut into 5 slices
Fresh dill sprigs

① Spread about 1 tablespoon of Boursin on each bread round. Top each round with cucumber and tomato slices and garnish with dill.

② Cut off the crusts and cut into triangles or squares.

③ Place a damp paper towel over the tea sandwiches to keep them moist and fresh.

Mini BLT Tea Sandwiches

MAKES ABOUT 40 SANDWICH TRIANGLES

1 loaf sliced potato bread
1 cup Lulu's Special Sauce (page 168)
1 pound bacon, cooked, or Maple-
   Glazed Bacon (page 44), crumbled
8 plum tomatoes, thinly sliced

½ pound baby arugula
1 small red onion, thinly sliced
½ pound Boar's Head horseradish
   Cheddar cheese (optional)

① Lightly toast the bread.

② Spread a small amount of Lulu's Special Sauce on half of the bread slices, followed by a small amount of bacon.

③ Layer the tomatoes, arugula, onion, and cheese on top of the bacon and top with the remaining bread slices.

④ Cut the sandwiches into 4 triangles and serve.

Curried Chicken Salad with Endive

This makes a great salad with greens or an appetizer served on endive leaves.

MAKES 32 PIECES

¼ cup mayonnaise

¼ cup mango chutney

2 teaspoons curry powder

1 garlic clove, crushed

2 scallions, both white and green parts, thinly sliced

2 tablespoons chopped golden raisins

1½ teaspoons salt

½ teaspoon pepper

2 cups shredded cooked chicken

4 heads of Belgian endive

① In a large mixing bowl, combine the mayonnaise, chutney, curry powder, garlic, scallions, raisins, salt, and pepper and mix well. Add the shredded chicken and stir gently.

② Slice off the ends of the endive and gently pull apart the leaves. Spoon 1 tablespoon chicken salad into each leaf.

Apricots with Blue Cheese and Mint

This is another Powers family favorite. It's an easy, bite-sized appetizer. Substitute fresh apricots in the summer. Triple-cream Brie such as St. André makes a decadent stand-in for the blue cheese, which should be the moist, spreadable kind, not the kind you crumble.

1 cup soft blue cheese such as Cashel Blue

30 dried apricot halves

30 whole or julienned fresh mint leaves

Scoop a teaspoon of cheese into each apricot and top with a mint leaf or a few shreds. You can make these up to 8 hours ahead and refrigerate; just add the mint leaf right before serving. Make sure the apricots are at room temperature before serving so that the cheese has maximum flavor.

Rosemary Scones

I serve these scones with a tangy cream, a combination of whipped cream and sour cream, and sometimes with raspberry jam. I have even cut the scone in half, toasted it, put a scoop of vanilla ice cream on top, and garnished with some berries—puuurrfect!

MAKES 12 SCONES

½ cup cornmeal

1½ cups all-purpose flour

3 tablespoons sugar

2½ teaspoons baking powder

½ teaspoon salt

5 tablespoons unsalted butter, cut into pieces

¼ cup plus 2 tablespoons half-and-half

1 large egg, lightly beaten, plus 1 egg for egg wash

½ cup golden raisins

2 tablespoons orange zest

2 tablespoons chopped fresh rosemary

2 tablespoons milk

① Preheat the oven to 400°F. Line a baking sheet with a Silpat baking mat or spray it lightly with nonstick cooking spray.

② Combine the cornmeal, flour, sugar, baking powder, and salt in a bowl.

③ Place the dry ingredients in a food processor, add the butter, and pulse 4 or 5 times, until the mixture forms coarse crumbs. Return to the bowl. (If you don't have a food processor, use a pastry blender or 2 knives to cut in the butter.)

④ Add the half-and-half, egg, raisins, orange zest, and rosemary and mix lightly. (Do not overmix, or the scones will be tough.)

⑤ Turn the dough out onto a floured work surface and knead lightly until the dough clings together and is soft and puffy, about 1 minute.

⑥ Gently roll out the dough to a ¾-inch thickness.

⑦ Dust a 2¼-inch round biscuit cutter with flour and, using a quick, sharp motion, cut out the scones as close together as possible. Gather the scraps of dough, knead briefly, roll out, and cut additional scones. You can cut the scones out with smaller cookie cutters or a different shape. Hearts are fun for a wedding shower, or use a flower-shaped cookie cutter for a Mother's Day brunch. In a small bowl, beat together the remaining egg with the milk.

⑧ Place the scones 1½ inches apart on the baking sheet. Brush the scones with the egg wash using a pastry brush. Bake for 14 minutes, or until the edges are golden brown.

Deviled Eggs

Eggs are one of my favorite things to eat, and this appetizer is timeless. Deviled eggs are great for showers because you can prepare them ahead. Just garnish them right before you serve them.

MAKES 24

1 dozen eggs

2 teaspoons Dijon mustard

⅓ cup mayonnaise

1 tablespoon minced shallot

1 tablespoon sweet pickle relish

½ teaspoon Tabasco sauce

1 teaspoon apple cider vinegar

½ teaspoon salt

¼ teaspoon white pepper

1 teaspoon finely chopped fresh dill, plus sprigs for garnish

Paprika

① Place the eggs in a large pot filled with cold water and bring to a boil, uncovered. Turn off the heat, cover, and let stand for 11 minutes.

② Remove the eggs from the pot and immediately plunge them into an ice bath until the eggs are completely cool.

③ Remove the shells and slice the eggs in half lengthwise. Scoop out the yolks and place into the bowl of a food processor. Set the egg whites aside.

④ Add the mustard, mayonnaise, shallot, relish, Tabasco, cider vinegar, salt, pepper, and chopped dill to the food processor and pulse until smooth.

⑤ Spoon or pipe the egg mixture into the egg whites and garnish with dill sprigs and a dash of paprika.

Lulu's Tip

Before you cook the eggs, poke a hole in each end of the eggs with a pin and they'll be easier to peel after they're cooked.

Smoked Salmon with Scallion Crème Fraîche on Garlic Herb Crostini

MAKES ABOUT 30 PIECES

FOR THE SCALLION
CRÈME FRAÎCHE

1 cup crème fraîche or sour cream

One 8-ounce package cream cheese

4 scallions, both green and white parts,
 thinly sliced

1 shallot, minced

Zest of 2 lemons

Juice of 1 lemon

Pinch of sugar

Salt and pepper to taste

FOR THE GARLIC
HERB CROSTINI

1 tablespoon finely chopped fresh
 parsley

3 garlic cloves, minced

8 ounces (1 stick) salted butter, at room
 temperature

Salt and pepper to taste

1 baguette, sliced ¼ inch thick

One 8-ounce sliced package smoked
 salmon

Chopped fresh chives

① To make the scallion crème fraîche, combine all the ingredients in the bowl of a food processor and process until blended.

② Preheat the oven to 400°F. To make the crostini, cream together the parsley, garlic, butter, salt, and pepper. Place the bread slices on a sheet pan and brush each one with the butter mixture. Bake until lightly toasted, about 5 minutes. Let cool completely.

③ Spoon a small amount of the scallion crème fraîche onto each crostino. Place a small amount of smoked salmon on top and garnish with chives.

Green Beans with Burrata Cheese

Burrata is the most delicious cheese. It's a richer, creamier cousin to mozzarella. Ask your local cheese store to order it for you. If it's not available, use mozzarella, but leave it at room temperature so it's very soft. It's also great with prosciutto and melon or with some nice sliced tomatoes and fresh basil.

SERVES 4

1½ pounds green beans, preferably the skinny haricots verts, trimmed

1 tablespoon olive oil

3 garlic cloves, sliced

1 tablespoon unsalted butter

1 teaspoon grade A or B maple syrup

Salt and freshly ground pepper to taste

1 pound Burrata cheese, sliced and then torn into pieces

Balsamic Glaze (recipe follows), for garnish

① Blanch the green beans in boiling water until they reach the desired tenderness.

② Heat the oil in a saucepan over medium heat and sauté the garlic until lightly browned, a minute or so. Add the green beans, butter, and maple syrup. Reduce the heat to medium-low and stir to combine.

③ Turn off the heat, season with salt and pepper, and transfer the beans to a serving dish.

④ Toss the green beans first and then top with the Burrata. Finish with a drizzle of balsamic glaze. Serve warm or at room temperature.

Balsamic Glaze

1½ cups balsamic vinegar

Pour the vinegar in a small saucepan and boil on high heat for 3 to 5 minutes, or until it coats the back of a spoon. Store it in a container in the fridge for up to 1 month.

Grilled Citrus Chicken and Brown Rice Salad

I always prefer to make brown rice in a rice cooker with chicken broth and short-grain brown rice; otherwise it just doesn't come out. I cook my chicken in a grill pan, but you could use a store-bought rotisserie chicken as a substitute. You can also make a brown rice salad bar, serving each ingredient in a separate bowl so people can mix and match.

SERVES 6 TO 8

FOR THE MARINADE

½ cup fresh tarragon leaves

½ cup fresh cilantro, leaves and stems coarsely chopped, plus cilantro for garnish

5 garlic cloves

1 teaspoon Tabasco sauce

½ cup freshly squeezed lemon or lime juice

¼ cup grade A or B maple syrup

½ cup olive oil

2 teaspoons salt

½ teaspoon pepper

FOR THE SALAD

2 to 3 pounds boneless, skinless chicken breasts

4 cups short-grain brown rice

2 quarts chicken stock or water

¼ cup soy sauce

¼ cup olive oil

¼ cup orange juice

¼ cup freshly squeezed lemon juice

1 teaspoon sugar or grade A or B maple syrup

2 garlic cloves, crushed

4 caramelized leeks (see Note)

Salt and white pepper to taste

2 pints small cherry tomatoes (teardrop shaped if available)

2 bunches of scallions, both white and green parts, thinly sliced

2 bunches of fresh cilantro, roughly torn

1. Process all the marinade ingredients in a food processor or blender. Pierce the chicken breasts with a fork several times and place in a Ziploc bag along with the marinade. Marinate in the refrigerator for at least 1 hour and up to 24 hours before grilling.

2. Grill the chicken over medium-high heat for 5 minutes on each side.

3. Meanwhile, cook the rice in the chicken stock according to the package directions.

4. To make the dressing, whisk together the soy sauce, olive oil, orange juice, lemon juice, sugar, garlic, leeks, salt, and pepper.

5. When the rice is cooked and still warm, combine with the dressing and leeks and mix well. Either pull apart or slice the chicken and toss with the rice.

6. Serve with bowls of tomatoes, scallions, and cilantro. The salad can be served warm or at room temperature and be made up to 1 day ahead.

NOTE: Caramelized leeks are easy to make. Clean and thinly slice the leeks. In a sauté pan, melt 2 tablespoons of butter and sauté the leeks on medium-low heat along with 2 teaspoons sugar, $1/2$ teaspoon salt, and $1/4$ teaspoon pepper until the leeks begin to brown but not burn, about 15 minutes.

Lulu's Tip

Pour the salad dressing into a glass bottle with a pour top, which can be found at any kitchen store. Put a tag on the bottle telling guests what it is. You can also put out little bottles of balsamic vinegar and olive oil and salt and pepper and let guests make their own dressing.

Chocolate-Coconut Macaroons

These macaroons are easy to make. You can keep all the ingredients in your pantry. They're also nice to bring as a little hostess gift, with a note that includes the recipe written on the back.

MAKES 18

4 ounces semisweet or bittersweet chocolate, chopped
3 large egg whites
¼ cup unsweetened cocoa powder
⅛ teaspoon ground cinnamon

1 cup sugar
¼ teaspoon salt
¼ teaspoon vanilla extract
2½ cups unsweetened dried flaked coconut

① Preheat the oven to 325°F. Line 2 baking sheets with Silpat baking mats or spray lightly with nonstick cooking spray.

② In a stainless-steel bowl set over a pot of simmering water, melt the chocolate. Set aside.

③ Meanwhile, in a large bowl, whisk together the egg whites, cocoa powder, cinnamon, sugar, salt, and vanilla. Stir in the coconut and melted chocolate, making sure the coconut is well coated. If the mixture is too soft, refrigerate for 30 minutes before proceeding.

④ Using an ⅛-cup measuring cup, scoop the mixture into individual rounds and place them on the baking sheets a few inches apart. (If you have a pastry bag with a wide tip you can pipe the macaroons onto the baking sheets.)

⑤ Bake for 18 minutes, or until the macaroons are shiny.

⑥ Let the macaroons cool on the baking sheet for about 10 minutes and then transfer them to a wire rack to cool. Store in a Tupperware container for up to 1 week, layered with wax paper.

Strawberry Shortcakes with Maple Yogurt

This is my sweet sister Sarah's recipe from when we were kids working for Sarah Leah Chase at her charming shop on Nantucket.

SERVES 6

2¼ cups all-purpose flour
½ cup plus 1 tablespoon sugar
1½ teaspoons baking powder
¾ teaspoon baking soda
½ teaspoon salt
6 tablespoons (¾ stick) butter, chilled
and cut into pieces
⅔ cup buttermilk
1 large egg yolk

½ teaspoon vanilla extract
⅛ teaspoon almond extract
3 tablespoons heavy cream
⅓ cup sliced almonds
1 pint strawberries, hulled and sliced
Maple yogurt (available at most
grocery stores) or Whipped Cream
(page 145)

1. Preheat the oven to 425°F. Line a sheet pan with parchment paper or spray with baking spray.

2. Put the flour, ½ cup sugar, baking powder, baking soda, and salt into a food processor and pulse to combine. Add the butter and process until the mixture forms crumbs.

3. Whisk the buttermilk, egg yolk, and vanilla and almond extracts together in a small bowl. With the food processor running, pour the buttermilk mixture through the feed tube and process until the dough is somewhat sticky.

4. Transfer the dough to a floured sheet of wax paper. Gently pat the dough to an even ¾-inch thickness. Do not handle the dough too much. Using a 3-inch cookie cutter, cut out 6 circles and place on the sheet pan.

5. Brush each circle with heavy cream and sprinkle a spoonful of almonds on top of each. Sprinkle the circles with the remaining 1 tablespoon sugar.

6. Bake for 12 to 13 minutes, or until light golden brown. When cooled, split the cakes in half with a knife. Fill with a spoonful of sliced strawberries and maple yogurt.

Lulu's Fresh Mint Tea

You can serve it plain or add maple syrup (my husband's favorite), fresh ginger, or even lavender syrup. It's my own version of Moroccan tea.

1 handful fresh mint leaves

Let the mint leaves steep in 1 quart hot water for 10 minutes. You can also chunk up fresh ginger and add honey or maple syrup to make a Moroccan version. It can be served hot or iced. You can make it ahead and reheat it in a microwave.

The Phil Mickelson

My husband made up this drink and decided to name it after the golfer Phil Mickelson. He also refers to it as "the younger Arnold Palmer."

SERVES 1

½ cup any unsweetened iced tea such as Paradise brand Tropical Tea (see Note)
½ cup cranberry juice
1 thin slice lime or kiwi

Fill a tall glass with ice and add the iced tea and cranberry juice. Stir, garnish with a lime slice, and serve.

NOTE: I really like this tropical tea, and I always keep it on hand in my fridge. This tea is also good mixed with lemonade or any juice you have on hand.

Lulu's Tip

Try maple syrup instead of sugar to sweeten your iced tea. Add a sprig of mint or a few apple slices to garnish.

SUNDAY LUNCH PROVENÇAL

Growing up, my sisters, brother, and I had to be home—and dressed up—for Sunday night dinner. A collared shirt and skirt were required—no pants allowed except for my brother. Sunday night dinner was the only time we could all sit down together. With everyone's hectic schedules, few people have the chance to eat with their family, but a relaxing Sunday lunch is a perfect time to get together.

In France, Sunday lunch is the designated time to see family, and this menu will suit both the palates and schedules of busy families. I've been lucky enough to experience the real thing. My sister Sue, who lived in Paris for ten years, rented a house in Provence every summer and invited the Powers clan to visit. How could we turn down an invitation like that? I fell in love with two towns in the south of France: Cavaillon and Monflanquin. Every morning we would shop at a different outdoor food market in neighboring towns, buying tomatoes, herbs, cheese, bread, and roasted chickens as well as bunches of fresh flowers. When we got home, we sliced the tomatoes and put out the chicken along with whatever other goodies we found: olives, *saucissons* (French sausages), and cheeses.

There are plenty of shortcuts for this menu. You can add a glaze (see page 128) to a preroasted chicken and make the roasted vegetables and the dessert the day before. This menu can be used for a great Sunday dinner as well—it's really an anytime Sunday meal.

Lulu's Tip

I love cheese plates with lots of accoutrements. I serve room-temperature cheese with fresh baguette slices, honey, nuts, olives, cornichons, apricots, grapes, strawberries, prosciutto, breadsticks . . . it's up to you.

Make-Ahead Tips

Put the cheeses out on a cutting board the morning of the lunch. (Cheese should always be served at room temperature; it has much more flavor than when it's cold. The same goes for fruit, such as melons or berries.) Place bowls on the table filled with olive oil and balsamic vinegar mixed with crushed garlic and any chopped fresh herbs you like for dipping bread, along with a bowl of olives and a little bowl next to it for pits. You can dress up ordinary olives with some fennel seeds, red pepper flakes, and lemon or orange zest or even a pinch of herbes de Provence. Leave a plate of butter out at room temperature for guests to spread on a slice of baguette, alongside a small bowl of salt (see Sources for my favorite artisanal salts).

DÉCOR

For a Sunday lunch, a bunch of fresh flowers is the simplest way to set the table. If available, buy big bunches of lavender. Whether fresh or dried, lavender is aromatic and looks great.

Lemons are popular in the south of France, appearing in dishes and in decorations. I place big bowls of lemons on the table, and it's even better if you can find lemons with the leaves attached. If you have Provençal-style table-cloths and napkins, use them to create an authentic, relaxed feel. Deep blue and bright yellow are the traditional colors of the region, so use dishes in those colors if you can. Set the table with long baguettes, bowls of olives, and bottles of rosé wine.

Leek and Onion Tart

Nothing tastes better than sautéed leeks and onions. When you add the pastry dough, you've got a home run. This is great laid out for a buffet on a cutting board or served with a green salad. My friend Leslie gave me this recipe. Her little trick is to prep it the day before and leave it in the fridge until the party. She starts to bake it 5 minutes before the guests arrive so that delicious smells waft through the air.

SERVES 10

1 sheet puff pastry (half 17-ounce package; I use Pepperidge Farm), thawed

2 tablespoons olive oil

3 medium leeks, both white and green parts, cleaned, split lengthwise, and thinly sliced

1 medium sweet onion, thinly sliced

3 garlic cloves, sliced

1 teaspoon salt

½ teaspoon white pepper

1 teaspoon sugar

1 teaspoon fresh thyme leaves

1 cup grated Gruyère cheese

① Preheat the oven to 400°F.

② Roll out the puff pastry to fit a sheet pan (any size will do). Fold in the edges over ¼ inch to make a crust and place the pan in the refrigerator.

③ In a medium sauté pan over medium heat, heat the olive oil. Add the leeks, onion, and garlic and sauté for about 5 minutes, or until the onion is translucent. Add the salt, pepper, sugar, and thyme.

④ Remove the puff pastry sheet from the refrigerator.

⑤ Place a thin layer of the leek mixture on the puff pastry, followed by a thin layer of Gruyère. Continue to alternate layers until the mixtures run out.

⑥ Bake for about 20 minutes, or until the puff pastry is golden brown. Serve warm or at room temperature.

Lavender-Glazed Roasted Chicken

If you don't have time to roast the chicken yourself, just buy a roasted chicken at the market and brush it with a glaze of lemon juice, honey, lavender, salt, and pepper before reheating in the oven. Fennel seeds can be substituted for the lavender—add what you love.

SERVES 4

One 4- to 5-pound whole chicken
1 large lemon, cut in half
6 garlic cloves, thinly sliced
10 fresh rosemary sprigs
¼ cup orange juice

2 tablespoons Lawry's Seasoned Salt
1 teaspoon dried lavender, crumbled
  with your hand
¼ cup honey
¼ cup chicken stock

① Preheat the oven to 400°F.

② Rinse the chicken in cold water and pat it dry. Place it in a roasting pan and rub the lemon halves all over it, squeezing the juice onto the skin. Stuff the cavity with the lemons. (You can also cut up an apple and place it in the cavity for an even juicier, more flavorful chicken.)

③ Loosen the skin from the breast meat and stuff each side with the garlic slices and rosemary sprigs.

④ Flip the chicken breast side down and sprinkle with half of the orange juice, Lawry's Seasoned Salt, lavender, and honey.

⑤ Pour the stock into the pan and roast for 15 minutes, basting periodically.

⑥ Flip the chicken breast side up and season with the remaining orange juice, Lawry's Seasoned Salt, lavender, and honey. Roast for 45 minutes more, or until golden brown.

⑦ Let the chicken rest for 20 minutes before carving. Serve along with the juices from the pan.

JUST AN IDEA: Get creative with this glaze; try orange juice with brown sugar and cumin.

Lulu's Tip

For a quick and crispy roasted chicken, combine apricot jam and chicken broth and brush on the outside of a preroasted chicken. Roast for 10 minutes in a 400°F oven.

Herb-Marinated Lamb Chops

When I made these lamb chops for Madonna, I used lamb from Doheny Kosher Meat Market in Los Angeles.

SERVES 6

FOR THE MARINADE
1 cup fresh mint leaves
½ cup fresh parsley leaves
½ cup fresh rosemary leaves
½ cup freshly squeezed lime juice
5 garlic cloves
¼ cup grade A or B maple syrup
½ cup extra virgin olive oil

1 teaspoon Tabasco sauce
2 teaspoons salt
½ teaspoon freshly ground black
   pepper

2 racks of lamb, cut into individual
   chops (about 3 pounds)

① Place all the marinade ingredients in the bowl of a food processor and blend.

② Pierce the skin of the lamb chops with a fork several times and place them in a Ziploc bag. Pour three-quarters of the marinade over the lamb and marinate in the refrigerator for at least 1 hour and up to 24 hours.

③ Remove the lamb from the refrigerator at least 15 minutes before grilling.

④ Grill the lamb over medium heat for 2 to 3 minutes per side for medium-rare, or until a thermometer registers 140°F, using the remaining marinade to baste the lamb. If you don't have a grill, use a grill pan or a broiler heated on high.

Roasted Tomatoes

These tomatoes can be put out as a side dish or served over penne or linguine with some spinach. (Baby spinach will wilt perfectly on hot pasta without precooking.) In the summer, serve fresh tomatoes, sliced, with basil. Try adding different flavored salts or fennel seeds.

SERVES 6

6 large plum tomatoes or any tomatoes you have on hand, halved
Herbes de Provence to taste
2 tablespoons extra virgin olive oil
Salt and pepper to taste

1. Preheat the oven to 375°F.

2. Toss the tomato halves with a spoonful of herbes de Provence, olive oil, salt, and pepper and arrange them on a lightly oiled baking sheet.

3. Roast until the tomatoes become soft and the skins begin to blister, 15 to 20 minutes. Serve hot or at room temperature.

Roasted Asparagus

I make many variations of asparagus, but this is my basic recipe. Because I'm obsessed with truffle salt, I always sprinkle a little on top, along with some goat cheese and sometimes a fried egg.

SERVES 6 TO 8

2 bunches (about 2 pounds) of medium asparagus
2 tablespoons extra virgin olive oil
1 teaspoon truffle salt or Maldon sea salt
Freshly ground black pepper to taste

1. Preheat the oven to 400°F.

2. Break each asparagus spear with your hands where it naturally breaks, discarding the woody bottom stalk.

3. Wash and dry the asparagus spears, placing them in a single layer on a cookie sheet covered with foil or a Silpat baking mat. Drizzle with olive oil to coat the asparagus and add 1 teaspoon water.

4. Roast for 10 minutes (6 minutes if the asparagus are pencil-thin), shaking the pan once after 5 minutes.

5. Sprinkle the truffle salt over the top and add pepper to taste.

Truffle–Fingerling Potato Salad

I created this dish for a dinner I did for the writers of the television show "Six Feet Under." There was a container of crème fraîche and a bottle of truffle oil sitting on the counter, so I threw them in on a whim, and the result was delicious. This recipe seems fancy but is a breeze to make.

SERVES 8

4 pounds fingerling potatoes, sliced in half lengthwise

1 teaspoon extra virgin olive oil

4 tablespoons (½ stick) salted butter, cut into small pieces

One 7.5-ounce container crème fraîche

½ cup finely chopped fresh chives

2 tablespoons truffle oil

1 teaspoon salt

½ teaspoon white pepper

Pinch of sugar

① Preheat the oven to 400°F.

② On a sheet pan, toss the potatoes with olive oil and scatter the pieces of butter on top.

③ Roast for 20 to 25 minutes, or until the potatoes are fork-tender.

④ Transfer the potatoes to a mixing bowl and let cool for 5 minutes.

⑤ In a medium bowl, combine the crème fraîche, chives, truffle oil, salt, pepper, and sugar. Toss the mixture with the potatoes until well coated. Serve warm or at room temperature.

Mini Apple Tarts

These are great because they can be made a couple of days beforehand. They have a delicious buttery crust that lends itself to more than just apples; peaches, strawberries, or chocolate mousse with caramel would also be delicious.

SERVES 12

FOR THE DOUGH
2 cups all-purpose flour

1 teaspoon salt

2 teaspoons granulated sugar

½ pound (2 sticks) salted butter, chilled and cut into pieces

FOR THE APPLES
2½ pounds Granny Smith apples, peeled, cored, and cut into 16 equal pieces

2½ teaspoons freshly squeezed lemon juice

2 teaspoons ground cinnamon

½ cup plus 2 tablespoons granulated sugar

2½ tablespoons salted butter, cut into small pieces, at room temperature

FOR THE WHIPPED CREAM
1 cup heavy cream

1 tablespoon confectioners' sugar

1 teaspoon ground cinnamon

① Preheat the oven to 400°F. Line a baking sheet with a Silpat baking mat.

② In a food processor, combine the flour, salt, and granulated sugar until blended. Add the chilled butter and pulse until the mixture resembles crumbs. Add up to ¼ cup ice water and pulse until the dough just comes together when pinched with your fingers.

③ Place the dough on a lightly floured surface and gently knead together with your hands. Wrap in plastic and refrigerate for at least 1 hour before rolling out the dough.

④ Remove the dough from the refrigerator and roll out onto a lightly floured surface until the dough is approximately ⅛ inch thick. Using a 3½-inch round biscuit cutter, cut out 12 rounds. Prick each round with a fork and partially bake them on the sheet pan for 8 minutes. Let cool on the sheet pan.

⑤ Meanwhile, to prepare the apple filling, in a large bowl, toss the apples with the lemon juice, cinnamon, and granulated sugar.

⑥ Place in a baking dish and dot the top with small pieces of butter.

⑦ Bake for 45 to 50 minutes, or until the sugar-cinnamon mixture has begun to caramelize and thicken and the apples are cooked through. Remove from the oven and cool in the pan, stirring occasionally.

8. To assemble, arrange the apples on each pastry round, covering the entire surface and spooning a little of the juices left in the pan over each.

9. Bake for 10 to 12 minutes, or until light golden.

10. Meanwhile, prepare the whipped cream. In a mixer or food processor, whip the cream, confectioners' sugar, and cinnamon until firm peaks form.

11. Serve the tarts topped with a dollop of whipped cream.

NOTE: The tarts can be prepped 1 day ahead and assembled right before baking.

Lavender Lemonade

This is even great with a shot of citrus vodka.

MAKES 1 QUART

2 cups sugar
¼ cup dried lavender buds
2 cups freshly squeezed lemon juice (about 12 lemons)

1. Combine 1¾ cups water and the sugar in a large saucepan.

2. Rub the lavender buds in your hands to break them apart over the saucepan and into the water.

3. Turn the heat to medium-high and bring the water to a simmer. Simmer, stirring, for 3 minutes.

4. Remove from the heat and let steep for exactly 3 minutes (no longer or it will be become bitter).

5. Strain the lavender mixture through a fine-mesh strainer into a pitcher. Let cool.

6. Add the lemon juice and stir.

Lulu's Tip

If you have a lot of extra lemons, juice them, freeze the juice in ice cube trays or in small Ziploc bags and pull them out as needed.

WINTER PICNIC

When it's freezing outside and everyone's had it with winter, throw a picnic to perk up the mood. Even in Los Angeles, where winter basically means a few rainy days, it's fun to curl up in the living room on a gray day and relax.

This party was inspired by my dad, who prepared two different soups and sandwiches every Saturday for lunch, rain or shine. It made for a long, leisurely afternoon with friends dropping by for a bowl of soup and a chat. The soups changed every week, according to my father's culinary whims, which inspired my freewheeling cooking style. He made two different kinds of hero sandwiches, anything from roast beef and onion to mortadella with a sweet vinegar dressing. In the summer, he made onion, tomato, and basil sandwiches with ingredients from his garden.

This is an effortless party. Just pile wool blankets on the sofa and floor, light the fireplace, and invite people over for a casual picnic with their favorite comfort foods. Plaid blankets in particular make me think of tailgates and winter picnics. Serve the soups and drinks in Thermoses, wrap up sandwiches in deli paper or newspaper, and relax in the living room. Pull out your old-school games like chess, backgammon, and checkers to play after lunch.

DÉCOR

If you don't have a fireplace, light dozens of candles and place them around your living room to create a cozy, elegant effect. Get the picnic all set up before your guests arrive. An outdoorsy-smelling candle might get the mood going. Have everyone sit on the floor around low coffee tables. Or, if you have more space, set up game tables—card tables and chairs with a backgammon set or checkers on top.

Hero Sandwiches

Every weekend my beloved father made homemade soups and hero sandwiches. He made his usual trip to Peter's Market in Weston, Connecticut, for French bread, sandwich meats, and all the fixings for his soups. The sandwiches and soups varied according to the seasons, and my father had a flair for just about everything. He was my hero.

SERVES 6

1 loaf French bread
Mr. Powers's Hero Dressing (recipe
   follows)
1 pound Black Forest
   or honey-baked ham

½ pound thinly sliced sharp Cheddar
   cheese
1 small red onion, thinly sliced
1 tomato, thinly sliced
½ cup fresh basil leaves

1. Slice the loaf in half lengthwise and remove some of the interior.

2. Brush the inside of the loaves with the dressing.

3. Layer the ham, Cheddar, onion, tomato, and basil on one side of the bread.

4. Top with the remaining bread half. Slice and serve.

Mr. Powers's Hero Dressing

MAKES ABOUT 1 ½ CUPS

¾ cup extra virgin olive oil
½ cup red wine vinegar
1 teaspoon Dijon mustard
2 tablespoons chopped fresh
   flat-leaf parsley

1½ teaspoons dried oregano
2 tablespoons sugar
1 teaspoon salt
1 teaspoon freshly ground black pepper

Whisk all the ingredients together in a glass measuring cup. The dressing can be made up to 5 days ahead and stored in a sealed container; just whisk again briefly before using.

Roast Beef Hero

SERVES 6

1 loaf French bread
Horseradish Dressing (recipe follows)
1 pound sliced roast beef
½ pound pepperoni, thinly sliced

1 small red onion, thinly sliced
Leaves from 1 head of romaine lettuce
½ pound Boar's Head horseradish
    Cheddar cheese, thinly sliced

1. Slice the loaf in half lengthwise and remove some of the interior.

2. Brush the insides of the loaf with the dressing.

3. Layer the roast beef, pepperoni, onion, lettuce leaves, and cheese on one side of the bread.

4. Top with the remaining bread half. Slice and serve.

Horseradish Dressing

MAKES ABOUT ¾ CUP

½ cup mayonnaise
1 tablespoon prepared horseradish
2 garlic cloves, crushed
1 teaspoon sugar

1 teaspoon salt
½ teaspoon pepper
1 tablespoon extra virgin olive oil

Mix all the ingredients together until thoroughly combined. The dressing will keep in a sealed container in the refrigerator for 1 week.

The Ritz Tomato Soup

One of my clients said, "This tastes just like the tomato soup at the Ritz in Paris."

SERVES 6

1 onion, chopped
1 tablespoon extra virgin olive oil
2½ pounds plum tomatoes, chopped, or cherry tomatoes
½ cup chopped carrot
5 garlic cloves, chopped
3 bay leaves

2 cups chicken stock
¼ cup dry white wine
2 teaspoons salt
¼ teaspoon pepper
2 teaspoons sugar
Mascarpone cheese
Fresh basil leaves, julienned

1. In a medium sauté pan over medium heat, sauté the onion in the olive oil until translucent, about 5 minutes. Add the tomatoes, carrot, and garlic and sauté until the tomatoes are soft and beginning to fall apart, about 10 minutes.

2. Add the bay leaves, chicken stock, white wine, salt, pepper, and sugar. Simmer for 25 to 30 minutes over low to moderate heat.

3. Remove the bay leaves and puree with a hand blender or transfer to a blender and puree. Adjust the seasonings as desired.

4. Serve with a dollop of mascarpone and julienned basil.

Mr. Powers's Broccoli Soup

This recipe was first published in Sarah Leah Chase's *Cold-Weather Cooking*. My father was a creative cook just like me, adding a little of this and a little of that. When my friend Jenny Morton saw this recipe, she said, "I now understand where you inherited your way of cooking." Who would think to add mustard seeds? My father, of course.

SERVES 6

6 tablespoons (¾ stick) unsalted butter
2 medium onions, minced
2 large potatoes, peeled and diced
1 large bunch of broccoli, trimmed and chopped
6 cups chicken stock

Salt and freshly ground black pepper to taste
1 cup heavy cream
¼ cup mustard seeds
1 cup grated Parmesan cheese

① Melt the butter in a stockpot over medium-high heat.

② Add the onions and sauté until soft and translucent, about 10 minutes.

③ Stir in the potatoes and broccoli, cover with chicken stock, and season with salt and pepper. Add the cream and stir. Cook for 15 minutes over medium-high heat.

④ Transfer the soup to the bowl of a food processor or blender and puree. (I also love hand immersion blenders to blend soup in the pot.)

⑤ Return the soup to the pot and stir in the mustard seeds and Parmesan. (If the soup seems too thick, thin it with some milk.) Reheat the soup if needed and serve hot.

NOTE: The mustard-seed flavor becomes more pronounced as the soup sits, so you may want to make the soup a day or so in advance.

Parmesan Toasts

These little toasts can accompany many things, from soups to salads or just a cheese plate. They're also great right out of the oven.

MAKES 20 PIECES

8 tablespoons (1 stick) unsalted butter, at room temperature

4 garlic cloves, minced or put through a garlic press

¼ cup finely chopped fresh parsley or another favorite herb

1 teaspoon lemon zest

½ teaspoon salt

¼ teaspoon pepper

1 teaspoon freshly squeezed lemon juice

1 sourdough baguette, cut into ¼-inch slices

½ cup grated Parmesan cheese

① Preheat the oven to 400°F. Line a baking sheet with a Silpat baking mat or spray with nonstick cooking spray.

② In a small bowl, cream together the butter, garlic, parsley, lemon zest, salt, pepper, and lemon juice.

③ Generously spread the butter mixture onto the bread slices.

④ Dip the buttered side of each bread slice lightly in the Parmesan and place it on the baking sheet.

⑤ Bake for 8 minutes, or until lightly golden brown.

JUST AN IDEA: Add ½ teaspoon Tabasco sauce or ½ teaspoon poppy seeds to the butter mixture to add a zing.

Mr. Powers's Potato Salad

This recipe appeared in Sarah Leah Chase's *Nantucket Open-House Cookbook*. It's one of only two recipes my father wrote down, because he cooked by the seat of his pants!

SERVES 14 TO 16

FOR THE SALAD

4 pounds small Red Bliss potatoes, scrubbed

1 cup heavy cream

1 cup chicken stock

½ cup dry white wine

1 bunch of scallions, both white and green parts, chopped

1 medium red onion, minced

1 cup minced fresh parsley

Salt and freshly ground black pepper to taste

FOR THE VINAIGRETTE

1 cup sherry vinegar

2 teaspoons dry mustard

1 teaspoon dried thyme

1 cup extra virgin olive oil

Salt and freshly ground black pepper to taste

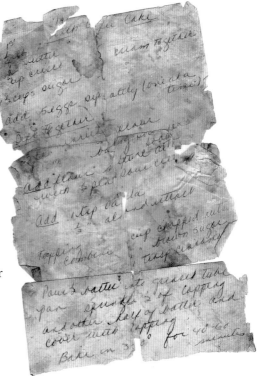

1. Place the potatoes in a large pot and add water to cover. Bring to a boil, lower the heat, and simmer, uncovered, until the potatoes are fork-tender, about 25 minutes.

2. Drain in a colander. Using a serrated knife, slice the potatoes about ½ inch thick.

3. Cover the warm potato slices with the cream, chicken stock, and wine in a large bowl. Marinate for 30 minutes and then pour off any excess liquid.

4. For the vinaigrette, whisk the vinegar, mustard, and thyme together in a medium bowl. Whisk in the oil and season with salt and pepper.

5. Pour the vinaigrette over the potatoes and toss to combine.

6. Add the scallions, onion, and parsley to the salad and toss to combine. Taste and adjust the seasonings.

7. Serve the salad warm or at room temperature.

Espresso Snowballs

This dessert is as fun as it is decadent. I like to use strongly flavored coffee ice cream, such as Starbucks or Double Rainbow brand, but feel free to use your favorite flavors. Around the holidays, use peppermint ice cream instead. I've included my chocolate sauce recipe, but you can use caramel sauce instead if you prefer.

MAKES 16 SNOWBALLS

FOR THE SNOWBALLS
1 quart ice cream
1 bag (7 ounces) sweetened dried flaked coconut

FOR THE CHOCOLATE SAUCE
12 ounces semisweet chocolate chips
4 tablespoons (½ stick) unsalted butter
1 tablespoon instant espresso powder

1. Preheat the oven to 400°F.

2. Tightly cover a jelly-roll pan with plastic wrap.

3. Using an ice cream scooper dipped in hot water, scoop the ice cream into rounded balls and place them on the plastic wrap. Freeze the ice cream balls for 1 hour.

4. In the meantime, spread the coconut on a cookie sheet and bake for 5 minutes, or until toasted, stirring frequently and checking often to make sure it's not burning. Let cool and transfer to a wide, shallow bowl.

5. Remove the snowballs from the freezer. Roll each ball in the toasted coconut, lay it back on the jelly-roll pan, and freeze until ready to serve. (They will keep uncovered for 1 day or covered with plastic wrap for up to 5 days.)

6. To make the chocolate sauce, in a medium saucepan, melt the chocolate chips, butter, espresso powder, and 1 tablespoon water over low heat, stirring constantly until melted and combined. (You can substitute your favorite jarred chocolate sauce if you prefer.)

7. To serve, remove the snowballs from the freezer. Spoon the chocolate sauce onto each serving plate or bowl until the bottom is covered and place a snowball on top.

S'Mores

I made my first s'mores around a bonfire on the beach in Nantucket. But you don't need a bonfire to make these gooey treats. You can buy individual hibachis at housewares stores, hang metal skewers in the fireplace, or use the broiler.

SERVES 8

1 package (10 ounces) large marshmallows
1 package (14.5 ounces) graham crackers (cinnamon or plain)
10 Hershey's milk chocolate bars
Skewers (see Note)

If you're using a fireplace or hibachi, thread the marshmallows on the skewers and place them over the flame until golden. Place 1 marshmallow on 1 graham cracker half, place the desired amount of chocolate on top, and top with another graham cracker half if desired.

If you're using a broiler, break each graham cracker in half. Place the graham crackers on a single layer on a baking sheet or piece of aluminum foil. Place 1 marshmallow on each cracker. Broil for 3 minutes, watching carefully to make sure they don't burn. Remove the baking sheet from the oven and place the desired amount of chocolate on top. Top with another cracker half if desired. (For smaller, bite-sized s'mores, cut the crackers into quarters and top with half a marshmallow and 1 square of chocolate.)

NOTE: If using wooden skewers soak them in water for at least 30 minutes.

Billie's Hot Chocolate
with Reese's Peanut Butter Cups

My friend Jenny Morton has a restaurant in Santa Monica, California, called the Blue Plate, where she serves this hot chocolate. Her daughter, Billie, always likes to put a peanut butter cup in the bottom of her hot chocolate cup, and that's where the name came from.

My favorite hot chocolate is Mexican, and I like it with a shot of Frangelico and a dollop of whipped cream.

SERVES 6

5 ounces bittersweet chocolate

6 cups whole milk

¼ cup sugar

2½ teaspoons ground cinnamon

⅛ teaspoon cayenne (optional)

Reese's Peanut Butter Cups

Whipped Cream (recipe follows)

① Melt the chocolate in a double boiler or in a stainless-steel bowl set on top of a pot of simmering water.

② Pour the milk into a medium saucepan and add the sugar, cinnamon, and cayenne. Heat over low heat until simmering.

③ Whisk a cup of the milk into the chocolate. Add the chocolate mixture to the milk mixture and whisk until smooth.

④ To serve, place one Reese's Peanut Butter Cup in the bottom of each mug and ladle the hot chocolate into the mugs. Top with a spoonful of whipped cream.

Whipped Cream

1 cup heavy cream

1 teaspoon pure vanilla extract

Whip the cream and vanilla together with a mixer or food processor until stiff.

Chocolate-Cranberry-Oatmeal Cookies

MAKES 72

4 cups old-fashioned rolled oats
2 cups all-purpose flour
½ cup toasted wheat germ
1 teaspoon baking soda
1 teaspoon baking powder
½ teaspoon ground cinnamon
½ teaspoon salt
2 cups packed light brown sugar

½ pound (2 sticks) butter, softened
8 tablespoons (1 stick) margarine, softened
2 large eggs
1 teaspoon vanilla extract
2 cups semisweet chocolate chips
1 cup dried cranberries

① Preheat the oven to 350°F. Line a baking sheet with a Silpat baking mat or spray with nonstick cooking spray.

② In a large mixing bowl, stir together the oats, flour, wheat germ, baking soda, baking powder, cinnamon, and salt and set aside.

③ Place the sugar, butter, and margarine in the bowl of an electric mixer and mix on medium speed until fluffy.

④ Beat in the eggs one at a time and then the vanilla.

⑤ Reduce the speed to low and slowly add the oat-flour mixture until just combined.

⑥ Add the chocolate chips and cranberries and mix gently with a spatula.

⑦ Scoop the dough into rounds and place them 1 inch apart on the baking sheet.

⑧ Bake for 12 to 14 minutes, or until golden and just set. Let the cookies cool on the baking sheet for 5 minutes. Remove from the pan and cool completely on racks. Repeat with the remaining dough. The cookies will keep in an airtight container for 7 days.

JUST AN IDEA: Instead of baking it, keep the dough in the freezer and treat yourself to a bite every once in a while.

THE ANYWHERE, ANYTIME CLAMBAKE

Nothing says New England like a good old-fashioned clambake. This is a modern clambake, with lobster rolls substituting for the classic clams (and clam chowder on the side). And it's versatile: this party can be thrown indoors or outdoors, and almost every dish can be made ahead.

The best clambake I ever attended was on Temperance Island, a private island in Connecticut owned by my sister Molly's in-laws, Susan and Sandy Kellogg, affectionately known as Su-Su and Pops. The Kelloggs grew up on the water, and they open their house from April to November. The first time I visited, I felt as if I were in a Norman Rockwell painting. Sitting on the big, wide porches, digging steamers outside the front door at low tide, and living without electricity sends you back in time. We pulled our own lobster traps and had a feast of fresh lobster, clam chowder, and fresh corn.

But you don't need to live by the water to enjoy a clambake. It can be just as much fun on a picnic table in the backyard or on a kitchen table. If you do want to serve the classic clambake (boiled lobsters, clams, corn, and potatoes), there are plenty of companies that will ship the ingredients, pot and all, so you can feast anywhere, anytime (see Sources). Many seafood shops also sell clambakes—ask your local fish store or gourmet grocery store. Otherwise, just order cooked lobsters from your local fishmonger or buy lobster meat. If you can't get lobster, substitute crabmeat and make crab rolls instead. You can find canned crabmeat year-round,

and most grocery stores carry it. I love any type of crab, including Dungeness, blue crab, and stone crab, but stay away from imitation crab, which is actually made with white pollock and is flaky with a bright orange color. Ask your fishmonger if you're not sure.

My favorite cocktail for a clambake is the Dark 'n' Stormy, a rum drink from Bermuda. I also serve buckets of beer, Coca-Cola in bottles, and chilled white wine or rosé to get guests in the summertime mood.

DÉCOR

You can make the party fancy or more low-key. For an indoor clambake, just cover the table with newspaper or brown butcher paper, put out plenty of red paper napkins, and arrange the food family style (except for the soup—have one person serve soup in the bowls and pass them around to the guests). Buy a bag of sand from a local hardware store or garden center and spread it down the center of a small table like a table runner, scatter a few seashells on top, and stick the utensils in colorful plastic buckets. (You can find shells at most party stores.) Decorate with any small potted plants that you can find in season. Use brown paper as a tablecloth and just recycle it after the meal. Or set a more formal table and serve the clam chowder as a first course and go from there. This party is adaptable for guests in black tie or blue jeans.

Entertaining on the Go: Picnics and Outside Venues

If you're having a clambake or any other party outside, here's a list of essentials:

* **Cold drinks**
* **Sun umbrellas**
* **Windshields**
* **Insect repellent**
* **Coolers**
* **Sunblock**
* **Games:** break out the horseshoes, badminton, croquet, and any other games that are suited to the beach or a lawn.
* **Blow-up pools:** if you can't make it to the water, bring the water to you. Inflatable pools add a surprise element to summer parties; kids can splash and adults can dip their feet in.
* If you have a swimming pool, buy six or seven inflatable balls and other pool games.

Lobster Rolls

The first time I made lobster rolls I was a private chef for Tommy and Linda Taylor on Nantucket. They were going away on a trip and asked me to pack them lobster rolls, a Caesar salad, and cookies for the plane. They called me from their plane to tell me the lobster rolls were a "ten," and these rolls have been a hit ever since. I like to brush the rolls with butter and toast them facedown in a pan.

SERVES 8

1 cup mayonnaise, or more to taste
¼ cup chopped fresh tarragon
3 garlic cloves, minced
2 shallots, minced
1 teaspoon sugar

Juice of 1 lemon
1 teaspoon salt
¼ teaspoon ground white pepper
4 cups (2 pounds) cooked lobster meat
8 hot dog buns, toasted

① In a medium bowl, combine the mayonnaise, tarragon, garlic, shallots, sugar, lemon, salt, and pepper.

② Place the lobster meat in a separate bowl and add as much of the mayonnaise mixture as you like. It's purely a matter of taste, so mix carefully and adjust the proportions as desired.

③ Spoon the lobster salad into the toasted hot dog buns.

Clam Chowder

My father made the best clam chowder, and I think this could be as good as his—a little port and sherry helps!

MAKES 8 CUPS; SERVES 6 TO 8

1 pound bacon, chopped

¼ cup extra virgin olive oil

1 bunch of fresh sage, stems removed

5 shallots, finely chopped

2 leeks, both white and green parts, thinly sliced

1 cup finely chopped onion

1 teaspoon sugar

1 cup finely chopped carrot

1 cup finely chopped celery

1 pound small red potatoes, scrubbed and diced

1 cup dry white wine

4 tablespoons (½ stick) unsalted butter

2 cups bottled clam juice

2 cups chicken stock

1 cup heavy cream

1½ teaspoons Old Bay seasoning

1½ teaspoons white pepper

1½ teaspoons Tabasco sauce

Juice of 1 lemon

3 bay leaves

1 tablespoon chopped fresh dill

1 teaspoon chopped fresh thyme

1 tablespoon chopped fresh basil

2 tablespoons Harvey's Bristol Cream sherry

2 tablespoons port

2 cups shucked fresh clams or four 6-ounce cans clams, drained

① In a large stockpot over medium heat, fry the bacon until crispy. Remove the bacon, drain on paper towels, and set aside.

② Add the olive oil to the bacon fat and fry the sage leaves for 2 to 3 minutes. Remove the sage and drain on paper towels; reserve.

③ In the same pot, cook the shallots, leeks, onion, and sugar over medium-high heat until crispy, stirring constantly, about 5 minutes.

④ Add the carrot, celery, potatoes, wine, butter, clam juice, and chicken stock and bring to a boil.

(5) Add the cream, Old Bay, pepper, Tabasco, lemon juice, bay leaves, dill, thyme, basil, sherry, and port and stir. Crumble in the bacon and sage. Bring the soup back to a boil, reduce the heat to low, and let simmer for 45 minutes, or until somewhat thick. Add the clams and simmer for 5 minutes. (It will thicken as it stands.)

(6) Serve warm. It tastes even better the second day when the flavors meld.

NOTE: This soup is better the next day because the flavors meld. If it thickens up overnight, add a bit of water, stock, or clam juice. A fun serving idea is to place small bottles of Harvey's Bristol Cream sherry at each place setting so people can spike their soup!

The Tastiest Coleslaw

My mother loves this recipe. She is a coleslaw aficionado. Everywhere she goes she orders a side of coleslaw.

SERVES 8

¼ cup mayonnaise

1 teaspoon Tabasco sauce

1 teaspoon sweet pickle relish

1 teaspoon honey

1 teaspoon mustard

¼ teaspoon ground white pepper

⅛ teaspoon salt

¼ teaspoon celery seeds

⅓ cup chopped walnuts

¼ cup finely chopped onion

¼ cup finely chopped celery

¼ cup finely chopped red bell pepper

¼ cup dried cranberries

5 cups shredded cabbage (4 cups green napa cabbage, 1 cup red cabbage)

Mix all the ingredients except the red cabbage together in a large bowl. Cover and refrigerate for at least 1 hour to allow the flavors to meld. Add the red cabbage right before serving, otherwise it will bleed.

Grilled Corn with Lime-Cilantro Butter

Sweet summer corn is the best. You can make variations of the cilantro butter with different herbs and use lemon juice. If the corn isn't too sweet, add a little bit of maple syrup to the butter.

SERVES 12

8 tablespoons (1 stick) unsalted butter, softened

1 tablespoon freshly squeezed lime juice

½ teaspoon lime zest

½ teaspoon sugar

½ teaspoon salt

¼ cup chopped fresh cilantro

12 ears fresh corn, shucked

1. Combine the butter, lime juice, lime zest, sugar, salt, and cilantro in a medium bowl and mix well.

2. Grill the corn on a medium-hot grill for 10 minutes, turning occasionally.

3. Transfer the lime-cilantro butter to a serving bowl and serve with the corn.

NOTE: Before grilling the corn, soak the unshucked corn in water. The heat will dry the silk, which will come off when you peel off the husks. Use a paper towel to rub off any remaining corn silk.

Nantucket Apple Squares

One summer evening I was going to my friend Sally Horchow's sunset beach picnic out in Eel Point on Nantucket. I was supposed to bring the dessert, and it was too late to run out and buy something, so I improvised with what I had on hand.

MAKES 12 SQUARES

8 tablespoons (1 stick) salted butter, softened

4 ounces cream cheese (half 8-ounce package), at room temperature

½ cup plus 1 tablespoon packed brown sugar

¾ cup all-purpose flour

1 teaspoon ground cinnamon

2 apples, cored and thinly sliced

① Preheat the oven to 400°F. Use the butter wrapper to grease an 8-inch square baking pan.

② In the bowl of a food processor, combine the butter, cream cheese, and the ½ cup brown sugar. Add the flour and cinnamon and pulse to combine.

③ Press the mixture into the pan and cover with the apples, allowing the slices to overlap slightly. Scatter the 1 tablespoon brown sugar over the top.

④ Bake for 45 minutes, or until the crust is golden and the apples are tender.

⑤ Let cool for at least 20 minutes and cut into squares.

NOTE: You can make the apple squares 2 days ahead. Store on the counter.

Fruit Skewers

This is a great way to serve fruit at a party, and it's easy to do ahead of time. You can use wooden skewers or even edible skewers such as rosemary branches. You might even add cayenne and a little spicy chile salt and a squeeze of lime to the fruit, as they do in the great fruit carts in downtown Los Angeles.

SERVES 8 (BUT IS EASILY DOUBLED)

Juice of ½ lemon or lime
Any fresh, ripe, seasonal fruit, cut into chunks: 1 mango, ½ cantaloupe, 1 cup chunked pineapple, 1 cup chunked watermelon, 1 pint strawberries

Pour the lemon juice over the fruit. Skewer the fruit on four 4-inch skewers; you could make miniature skewers with toothpicks; just cut the fruit into small pieces.

Limeade

This recipe is great for experimenting. You can mix this with rum, vodka, almost anything—use your imagination!

MAKES 2 QUARTS

2 cups sugar
1 quart freshly squeezed lime juice

1. In a large saucepan, combine the sugar and 3½ cups water and simmer over low heat until the sugar is dissolved, about 10 minutes.

2. Remove from the heat and let the mixture cool.

3. In a large pitcher, mix the sugar water with the lime juice. Serve cold.

JUST AN IDEA: Add a splash of club soda if you want to give the limeade some fizz.

Dark 'n' Stormy

I had my first Dark 'n' Stormy in Maine at my friend Bob Ireland's house, affectionately known as "The Ship." This drink is refreshing, and people seem to really like it. One of my clients, EGV, renamed the drink "the dirty rotten bastard." You gotta be careful, though—don't drink it like iced tea! It's fun to garnish it with a thin round slice of floating lime or kiwi.

SERVES 1

1½ ounces Gosling's Black Seal Rum or any other dark rum
Splash of bitters (optional)
About ½ cup ginger beer
½ lime

Fill a highball glass with ice, add the rum, a splash of bitters, if desired, and top with ginger beer. Squeeze the lime into the glass, stir, and add the lime to the drink.

INDEPENDENCE DAY CELEBRATION

The Fourth of July is a festive day, whether you're in the city, at the beach, or in a small town, and celebrating America's birthday is always a chance for a great summer bash. I've hosted tons of July 4 parties for my friends, as well as family gatherings on the East Coast, where we cook simple spreads and eat all day long.

Everyone in my family goes all out for this holiday. When I was young, we would gather at my aunt Patti Altman's house. She was a very creative hostess who made the whole day fun by instigating activities for the entire family, regardless of age. She organized races, treasure hunts, contests, and imaginative party favors like custom T-shirts for the guests, and she loved to pass out red, white, and blue Popsicles in Dixie cups. We called it Camp Altman, because every party was filled with a camp's worth of activities. We would walk down to the main street to watch the parade.

Wearing a boater hat, my dad would drive his red convertible in the local parade while the whole town looked on—dressed in red, white, and blue, down to the little girls' patriotic hair bows.

This is yet another example of a simple party. Bake "barbecued" chicken in the oven while you stick mozzarella, tomato, and basil on skewers (toothpicks adorned with flags or silver tinsel or rosemary sprigs make great skewers) and throw together a batch of Texas "Caviar" dip and finish the celebration with a gorgeous berry pound cake.

Plan the party around a local fireworks show to boost the patriotic spirit. If the fireworks are near a park or a beach, pack food in a basket, along with a blanket. And don't forget the drinks!

DÉCOR

Surprise your guests by serving bottled beer and soda in a wheelbarrow or a red wagon filled with ice. One year I set up an inflatable pool in my backyard, filled it with ice, and put bottles of Champagne, white wine, lemonade, Coca-Cola, water, and Pellegrino in it and juice boxes for the kids. I used Wite-Out to write HAPPY FOURTH on a red plastic ball and let it float in the pool. I stuck a flag behind the pool in an umbrella stand—another fun and festive touch.

For the cocktails, stick a mini American flag in each margarita. To liven up the dessert, place lit sparklers in the cobbler just before serving.

At this time of year you can find red, white, and blue streamers and banners, and you can hang them anywhere! Decorate the porch, bushes, and lawn with flags. Buy red, white, and blue cups and red or blue napkins. One year I used bandannas that said GOD BLESS AMERICA as napkins, and hung bunting on the front of the house. Flowers could include red, white, and blue gerbera daisies or blue delphiniums arranged in bunches or in buckets of sand. Even rosemary bunched with small flags looks festive.

Caprese Kebabs

These skewers are easy to assemble and make a wonderful summer dish.

SERVES 20

1 pint teardrop tomatoes
1 container mini mozzarella balls (*bocconcini*)
1 teaspoon extra virgin olive oil
½ teaspoon sugar
Salt and pepper to taste
1 bunch of fresh micro-basil leaves

① Slice the tomatoes and mozzarella in half horizontally. In a large bowl, toss the tomatoes with the olive oil, sugar, salt, and pepper.

② Thread half the tomatoes on toothpicks or small skewers, followed by half the mozzarella and then half the basil. Repeat with the remaining tomatoes, mozzarella, and basil.

③ Serve at room temperature.

Texas "Caviar" with Corn Chips

This spicy, chunky dip is what I call vegetarian "caviar." It's good ol' food, as they would say in Texas. My friend Ashley's mother, a Tennessee native, created something similar called "Tennessee caviar," so it must be a southern thing. It's addictive, so be careful!

SERVES 10

1 cup sugar

½ cup apple cider vinegar

½ cup extra virgin olive oil

One 15-ounce can pinto beans, drained and rinsed

One 15-ounce can black-eyed peas, drained and rinsed

One 14-ounce can white corn, drained and rinsed

One 4-ounce jar pimientos, drained, rinsed, and chopped

1 small red onion, chopped

1 green bell pepper, chopped

1 teaspoon finely chopped jalapeño pepper

1 teaspoon Tabasco sauce

2 tablespoons chopped fresh cilantro

2 tablespoons chopped fresh parsley

1 teaspoon salt

Tortilla chips (works best with Tostitos Scoops! or Fritos)

① Warm the sugar, vinegar, and olive oil in a small saucepan over medium heat until the sugar dissolves, 2 to 4 minutes. Let cool and set aside.

② In a large bowl, mix the pinto beans, black-eyed peas, corn, pimientos, red onion, green pepper, jalapeño, and Tabasco.

③ Add the sugar mixture and marinate for at least 2 hours. Drain and discard the liquid.

④ Add the cilantro, parsley, and salt and mix well.

⑤ Place the "caviar" in a serving bowl and serve along with the tortilla chips.

Aunt Patti's BBQ Chicken

One rainy Fourth of July, Aunt Patti taught me that you could use your oven to prepare "barbecued" chicken that looked and tasted as if it had just come off the grill.

SERVES 6 TO 8

3 pounds chicken wings and drumsticks
2 teaspoons garlic salt
½ teaspoon freshly ground black pepper
1 cup barbecue sauce (I prefer KC Masterpiece brand)
1 tablespoon finely ground espresso beans or Cafe Bustelo brand instant espresso
5 garlic cloves, minced

1. Preheat the oven to 400°F. Line a sheet pan with aluminum foil.

2. Rub the chicken with garlic salt and pepper and bake for 20 minutes. Turn the chicken over and bake for 20 minutes more. Remove from the oven and turn the oven to broil.

3. Combine the barbecue sauce, espresso, and garlic. Reserving a few tablespoons of sauce, brush one side of the chicken with the sauce and broil for 4 minutes. Remove, brush the other side, and broil for 4 minutes, allowing the chicken to char.

4. Remove the chicken and place on a platter. Brush with the remaining sauce before serving.

Fresh Watermelon Slices

Cut a watermelon in half and then into 1/2-inch-thick slices. Sprinkle the slices with sea salt and arrange on a serving platter. I like sprinkling lime juice and salt on my watermelon, along with a little cayenne.

Snow Pea Salad

I often made this refreshing summer salad while working for my mom in her catering business. It's a great staple. The dressing can be used on any salad.

SERVES 8

FOR THE SALAD

½ pound (1 cup) snow peas or sugar
   snap peas
1 large bell pepper (yellow, red, or
   orange), julienned
½ pound button mushrooms, sliced
2 tablespoons white or black sesame
   seeds, toasted

FOR THE VINAIGRETTE

3 tablespoons Champagne vinegar
1 tablespoon freshly squeezed lemon
   juice
1 tablespoon finely minced shallot
1 tablespoon sugar
½ teaspoon salt
¼ teaspoon ground white pepper
⅓ cup vegetable oil

① Remove the strings from the snow peas. Blanch them in a pot of boiling water for about 20 seconds, or slightly longer if you're using sugar snap peas. Drain the snow peas and immediately place them in an ice bath. When cool, drain again and set aside.

② To make the vinaigrette, in the bowl of a food processor, combine the vinegar, lemon juice, shallot, sugar, salt, and pepper. With the processor running, slowly add the oil through the feed tube until emulsified.

③ To assemble the salad, place the peas, bell pepper, mushrooms, and vinaigrette in a large bowl. Toss to combine and add the sesame seeds just before serving.

Lulu's Tri-Berry Pound Cake

Another one of Patty P's favorite desserts. Piled with fresh berries, this cake will impress anyone and is a great warm-weather dessert.

SERVES 12

FOR THE CAKE

8 tablespoons (1 stick) unsalted butter, at room temperature

½ pound (2 sticks) margarine, at room temperature

One 8-ounce package cream cheese

3 cups sugar

6 large eggs

3 cups all-purpose flour

1 tablespoon pure vanilla extract

FOR THE BERRIES

3 cups mixed berries (fresh or frozen)

3 teaspoons cornstarch

½ cup plus 1 tablespoon sugar

1 cup fresh blueberries for garnish

1 cup fresh raspberries for garnish

1 cup fresh strawberries, hulled and halved, for garnish

1 cup fresh blackberries for garnish

① Preheat the oven to 325°F. Butter and flour a Bundt pan.

② In the bowl of a mixer, mix the butter, margarine, and cream cheese until blended. Mix in the sugar and beat until light and fluffy.

③ Mix in 2 eggs, half the flour, then the remaining eggs, then the remaining flour, beating well after each addition. Add the vanilla and mix well.

④ Spoon the batter into the prepared pan and bake for 1 hour and 25 minutes, or until the top is golden brown.

⑤ Combine the mixed berries, cornstarch, sugar, and 2 tablespoons plus 1 teaspoon water in a medium saucepan over medium-high heat. Bring to a boil, lower the heat, and simmer, stirring occasionally, until the mixture begins to thicken, 3 to 4 minutes.

⑥ Place the cake on a serving platter. Pour the hot syrup over the cake. Spoon the fresh blueberries, raspberries, and strawberries over the top.

JUST AN IDEA: Instead of using berries, pile scoops of ice cream and spoonfuls of hot fudge or butterscotch in the middle of the cake.

Watermelon Lemonade

This is a refreshing drink for the afternoon, but if you want to serve it in the evening, add 2 ounces of your favorite vodka or tequila.

MAKES 2 QUARTS

4 cups chopped seedless watermelon
½ cup freshly squeezed lime juice
¼ cup sugar

FOR THE LEMON SYRUP
2 cups freshly squeezed lemon juice
1 cup sugar

1. Puree the watermelon, lime juice, and sugar in a blender until smooth.

2. To make the lemon syrup, combine the lemon juice, sugar, and 2 cups water in a small saucepan. Bring to a boil and stir until the sugar dissolves, 2 to 3 minutes. Let cool.

3. Mix the lemon syrup with the watermelon mixture. Serve over ice.

Margaritas

This is the ultimate margarita. I got the idea from my chef friend Christian's fortieth birthday party—his drinks are as good as his food.

SERVES 8

One 12-ounce can limeade
1 bottle Corona beer
12 ounces tequila (I use the limeade can to measure the tequila)
1 jigger Triple Sec

Mix the limeade, beer, tequila, and Triple Sec in a large pitcher. Add ice and stir. Serve from the pitcher or in 8 margarita glasses filled with ice.

JUST AN IDEA: For a fruity margarita, add 2 cups Watermelon Lemonade (above) and an additional 6 ounces (½ of a limeade can) tequila.

Lulu's Tip

This recipe also makes refreshing Popsicles. Just pour the mixture into Popsicle molds, add Popsicle sticks, and freeze for at least 1 hour. When you're expecting a crowd, make margaritas ahead of time in batches, so you can just pull them from the fridge.

THE BOWWOW BASH

Cheryl O'Leary, a true pet crusader, inspired this party. Every Easter in Palm Desert she throws a "bowwow" bash where people can bring their dogs. She greets every pooch with a collar wrapped in ribbons, and the dogs play or swim in the pool while their owners sip martinis.

These days dogs go everywhere with their human companions, so why not open up the house to the four-legged friends? Live the carefree life of a dog for the afternoon. Throw your own bowwow bash and invite your dog-loving buddies and your pals from the dog park over for drinks and snacks—with pooches welcome. If you don't have a backyard, plan the party at a local dog-friendly park or beach.

This is an afternoon snack-time party, complete with treats for the pups and their owners. Little burgers and homemade chips are both casual and easy to prepare, and dog-themed sweets make a fun ending to the meal. Bowls of water should be available for the pooches, but offer the owners a party cocktail. Bring out a big basket of dog toys for the canines to chew on and make blankets available for the dogs and their owners to sit on. This is a come-one, come-all party for dog lovers of all ages, from babies to grandparents.

PARTY FAVORS

Even the pups need something fun to take home with them. I like to prepare "doggy bag" party favors filled with colorful rawhide "lollipops," available at most pet food stores, or a selection of treats from a dog bakery (see Sources).

SHORTCUTS

To make quick and simple dog biscuit treats, buy five bags of mini bagels and put them in a big bowl for three days to let them harden. Voilà—instant dog biscuits at half the cost. Or make the pooches their own Frosty Paws (page 171). But for a real shortcut, visit a dog bakery and buy the treats. There are several dog bakeries around the country (see Sources) that make special treats for your four-legged friends.

Burger Bites with Lulu's Special Sauce

I've been a condiment queen my whole life. I love sauces! This sauce is even good for dipping with potato chips, and it's also good on any sandwich or hot dog.

MAKES 30 TO 35 BURGER BITES

FOR THE BURGERS

1 pound ground beef

3 tablespoons ketchup

3 tablespoons barbecue sauce

1½ teaspoons Lindberg-Snider Porterhouse and Roast Seasoning or other meat seasoning

2 teaspoons ground cumin

1 teaspoon ground black pepper

1 loaf sliced potato bread

FOR THE SAUCE

1 cup mayonnaise

2 teaspoons yellow mustard

2 tablespoons ketchup

1 tablespoon barbecue sauce

2 teaspoons Worcestershire sauce

2 teaspoons Tabasco sauce

2 tablespoons sweet pickle relish

2 teaspoons prepared horseradish

1 tablespoon freshly squeezed lemon juice

2 teaspoons sugar

1 teaspoon Lawry's Seasoned Salt

¼ cup chopped cornichons

2 tablespoons chopped peperoncini

4 garlic cloves

½ teaspoon ground white pepper

¼ cup chopped scallion, both white and green parts (optional)

① In a large bowl, mix the ground beef, ketchup, barbecue sauce, porterhouse seasoning, cumin, and pepper together until well incorporated.

② Shape the mixture into 1½-inch patties.

③ Roll out the bread with a rolling pin. Using a 1½-inch cookie cutter, cut 4 rounds out of each slice of bread and set aside.

④ Combine all the sauce ingredients in the bowl of a food processor and pulse until smooth.

⑤ In a sauté pan over medium-high heat, sear the patties for 1 to 2 minutes on each side for medium-rare, or until done to your liking.

⑥ Serve the burgers between 2 potato bread rounds, with a dollop of sauce on each patty.

Sweet Potato Chips

These homemade chips are delicious. Try using different kinds of salt on them. They're also great on a salad, with a sandwich, or even in a sandwich. I love them on my tuna sandwiches.

MAKES 80 CHIPS; SERVES 8

6 small sweet potatoes or yams, peeled and thinly sliced
Oil for deep frying, such as peanut, vegetable, or grapeseed
Salt to taste

1. Place the sliced potatoes in a bowl of ice water and set aside for 30 minutes. Drain and pat dry.

2. In a heavy, wide pot, heat 3 inches of oil to 375°F.

3. Put a handful of the potato slices in the oil, but do not crowd the pan. Fry until crisp and slightly golden, about 1 minute, stirring occasionally.

4. Remove the chips with a slotted spoon, drain in a single layer on paper towels, and season with salt. Repeat with the remaining potatoes.

NOTE: If you don't want to cook the potatoes immediately, you can keep them in a bowl of water in the refrigerator overnight. Drain them in a colander and dry well before frying. The chips can be made up to 6 hours ahead or stored in a sealed container for up to 2 weeks.

Tina's Tango

Bar none, this is my favorite cocktail. It's fresh, fruity, and flirty, introduced to me by my cousin Tina.

SERVES 1

2 ounces Absolut Citron or tequila
1 ounce freshly squeezed lemon juice
½ ounce Patrón Citrónge orange liqueur

Shake the ingredients in a cocktail shaker and serve on the rocks or strain and serve in a martini glass.

• FOR DOGS •

Frosty Paws

Dogs go crazy for these.

MAKES ABOUT 8 TREATS

2 cups yogurt
1 cup almond butter or sugar-free peanut butter
½ cup chopped carrots (optional)
8 thin rawhide dog chews

1. Combine the yogurt and almond butter in a large bowl and add the carrots, if using.

2. Spoon the mixture into small paper cups.

3. Place 1 rawhide chew in each cup, like a Popsicle stick.

4. Place the cups on a tray and freeze for 30 minutes.

5. Peel the Frosty Paws out of the cups and place them on a serving tray.

NOTE: These will keep in the freezer for up to 1 month. When you're ready to serve them, take them out of the freezer and let sit for 5 minutes. Then peel them out of the cups and place them on the serving tray.

Million-Dollar Bars

Taste just one of these treats and you'll understand the name. My mom's English friend, Mrs. Kennedy, introduced the Powers clan to Million-Dollar Bars. She wouldn't part with the recipe, so my sister Sarah and I came up with one ourselves. The problem is that you can't eat just one.

MAKES 35 BARS

1½ cups all-purpose flour

½ cup sugar

¾ pound (3 sticks) unsalted butter, 2 sticks chilled and cut into pieces, 1 stick at room temperature

½ cup packed brown sugar

Two 14-ounce cans unsweetened condensed milk

12 ounces semisweet chocolate chips

¼ cup heavy cream

1. Preheat the oven to 325°F.

2. Sift the flour into the bowl of a food processor. Add the sugar and the chilled butter and pulse until the mixture resembles crumbs.

3. Press the mixture into a 9 x 13-inch pan sprayed lightly with nonstick cooking spray and bake for 30 to 35 minutes, or until light golden. Let cool in the pan.

4. In a medium saucepan, melt the brown sugar and the remaining stick of butter. Add the condensed milk and stir constantly over medium-high heat until the mixture thickens slightly and becomes light golden in color, 3 to 4 minutes. Remove the caramel from the heat and pour evenly over the cooled cookie mixture. Let cool slightly.

5. In the meantime, melt the chocolate in a bowl over a pot of simmering water and gradually whisk in the heavy cream until smooth.

6. Pour the melted chocolate mixture over the caramel and spread it evenly with a small offset spatula or by tapping the bottom of the pan on a hard surface.

7. Cool the bars in the refrigerator until set and cut into squares. If the chocolate hardens, let the bars stand for at least 1 hour at room temperature before cutting. They will keep for 1 week on the counter and 2 weeks in the freezer.

Toffee Bark (Chocolate-Caramel Matzoh)

People go crazy over these; in fact, I have to hide them from my husband or he'll eat the whole batch. You can customize the bark by making it savory or spicy. My favorite toppings are cayenne and salt—I love the sweet, spicy, and savory combination.

MAKES ABOUT 2 POUNDS

4 to 6 unsalted matzoh crackers

¾ pound (3 sticks) unsalted butter

1½ cups packed brown sugar

1 cup semisweet chocolate chips (or any chocolate you desire)

¼ cup chopped nuts (optional)

¼ teaspoon cayenne (optional)

1 tablespoon flavored salt (such as tangerine or lavender) or plain ol' sea salt, the bigger the grain, the better (optional; see Sources)

① Preheat the oven to 350°F. Line a 12½ x 17½-inch jelly-roll pan completely with tinfoil. Place a Silpat baking mat or parchment paper on top of the foil.

② Place the matzohs in a single layer on the baking sheet, cutting or breaking them to fit if necessary. Be sure to cover the entire cookie sheet with matzohs.

③ In a saucepan, combine the butter and brown sugar. Cook over medium-high heat, stirring constantly, until the mixture comes to a boil. Cook for 3 minutes, stirring constantly. Remove the caramel from the heat and pour over the matzohs. (Be careful: This mixture becomes very hot. Don't even try to lick the spoon—you'll burn your tongue!)

④ Bake for 15 minutes, checking every few minutes to make sure the matzoh isn't burning, especially in the corners of the pan. If the edges are getting too dark, remove the pan from the oven, reduce the heat to 325°F, and then return the pan to the oven for the remaining time.

⑤ Place the pan on a cooling rack. Let sit for 2 minutes, then sprinkle the chocolate chips over the baked matzoh.

⑥ Let stand until the chips have melted—about 5 minutes—and then spread the melted chocolate over the caramel with an offset spatula.

⑦ While still warm, break the bark into pieces using a pizza cutter. Sprinkle the nuts, cayenne, and salt over the top if desired.

⑧ Chill the matzoh in the freezer, still in the baking sheet, until set, 30 to 60 minutes. Store the matzoh in a sealed container at room temperature for up to 3 days, although you won't have to because it will be eaten!

EVEN

ING

You don't have to have an occasion to celebrate to entertain—just think cocktails, food, flowers, good conversation, and fun. Although all the evening parties here are attainable, you can also just invite friends over for a last-minute dinner.

Don't be intimidated; the menu for an evening party can be as simple as a bowl of pasta or a grilled steak and a baked potato or as extravagant as a four-course meal. When you host a party, your guests will remember the party, not necessarily the food. It's more about creating a great vibe and an ambience than stressing about the hors d'œuvres or place settings. The most important thing, no matter whom you invite—whether it's your family, your neighbors, or your boss—is to make your guests feel special. Take the time and make sure to talk to everyone, even if it's just a brief welcome or "thanks for coming."

I cater for most of my clientele in the evening. I've seen it all—everything from an intimate dinner for two to a Grammy party for fifteen hundred. From caviar, blinis, Champagne, and seven-course dinners to cupcakes, hot dogs, and quesadillas, I try to give every party its own unique twist. As a host, just remember that the lighting, music, and décor set the tone more than anything else. It's worth spending extra time on the details to make the party seem effortless. If you see people laughing, eating, and having a good time, that's a successful party. I can't say it enough: the food is the least of your worries. As long as you have snacks and drinks ready, you're off to a good start. The trick is to be prepared.

I once taught a client to cook five things, and years later she told me she used those same recipes over and over for every party. Those were her staple dishes. If you're nervous, use basic recipes you're comfortable with and refer to the Parties R$_x$ chapter on page 5 for ideas. If it's your first foray into the world of entertaining, just invite a few friends over for dinner. They should be people you don't need to impress and who will just be glad to be there. Once your first party goes well, your confidence will increase, and gradually you'll invite more and more guests to your shindigs.

THE BIG CITY COCKTAIL PARTY

Whether they're long or short, cocktail parties are the most approachable way to entertain in the evening. Space, time, and money become less important if you think creatively. If a dinner party is like a relationship, then a cocktail party is like a fling—all the fun and none of the commitment.

My favorite kind of cocktail party is a "grazing" party, a term I picked up from my mother. I've used the term with my clients, who stare at me blankly. I know they're thinking of a cow in a field of grass. But to me grazing means serving a lot of wonderful foods people can sample—not just one or two appetizers but enough for guests to feel sufficiently full, as if they had dinner but didn't notice.

A "grazing" could go on for hours (a traditional cocktail party is two or three hours), and guests may or may not have somewhere else to go after the party. The best grazing I hosted started at 6:30 P.M., and we had to kick the last guest out at 1:30 A.M. Anybody can throw a grazing, whether in a small studio apartment or a spacious home, with a million-dollar or fifty-dollar budget. And don't panic about your space! You can host the liveliest, most decadent cocktail party without a lot of square footage.

If you're not quite up to a full-blown party, invite friends over for a drink to get your feet wet. When I tell people to "come for a cocktail," I

expect them to come for a visit for an hour or more, with no promises—which means I don't have to roll out the red carpet. In these instances, I set out a simple bowl of fabulous potato chips, some roasted nuts, and glasses of wine, Champagne, beer, or water. I invite people over for cocktails all the time because I have this party down to a science, and you can too—I promise. If your only skill is toasting bread, relax. With the shortcuts available in today's markets, you can pull together a great cocktail party with just a few key items. You don't need a bartender (although it would help to have one) or an army of servers. Just a few hours, some planning, and a few tricks, and you're ready to throw open the doors.

THE TIME LINE

Making the best use of your time will result in the most relaxing party for you and your guests. Start two lists: a grocery list and a drinks list. Write down what you plan to serve and then make a final shopping list. (If you're in the city, save yourself a step and have everything delivered.)

Food that can be made ahead is a lifesaver. You can bake ahead and freeze things like cookies, brownies, and even grilled cheese sandwiches. Roasted nuts will keep in a Tupperware container for weeks. Get a few things out of the way the night before: arrange a cheese tray and wash the grapes. Finish up basic host(ess) chores: arrange the candles and pull out the cocktail napkins. Stick some logs in the fireplace so all you have to do after work is buy a bag of ice and get the food out. And be sure to allow time for getting dressed; there's nothing worse than being half-dressed with dripping hair when the doorbell rings.

If you do find yourself in that situation, remember these hosting tips to get you through a party crisis: First, in any awkward situation, just smile and plow ahead. Your job is to make your guests comfortable no matter what, not to put them in the position of having to comfort you because you're a stress ball. Second, people just love to eat and drink. Open your home and give them a few treats and you'll already have made them happy. If you're not confident enough for this, take a deep breath, say, "I can do it," and then go get 'em.

> When you have guests who linger, there are a few subtle ways to tell them the party's over. Turning off the music, turning up the lights, and an "OK, guys, it's time for us to go to bed" usually does the trick. Or start cleaning up— they'll get the hint!

THE SPACE

Be creative with your space. You want to create flow. In the living room, push back any furniture that juts out. In the kitchen, clear the countertops to leave room for glasses and drinks. (And I mean *clear*: no vitamin bottles or telephone message pads! Put it all away.) Use your kitchen sink as a giant ice bucket: fill it with ice and add bottles of bubbly, wine, beer, and sparkling water for an instant bar. It's always nice to offer pitchers or bottles of water on some nice trays with glasses.

Have a garbage can or a big cardboard box lined with a garbage bag somewhere near the kitchen, so you can put all the dirty glasses in it and wash them later. That way your sink won't get cluttered and you won't have to keep opening the dishwasher. Always have nice plastic recyclable cups on hand as backup just in case you go through all your glasses. This is a must for your pantry. If you have a small kitchen and need more counter space, throw up a card table and put a tablecloth on it—you'll be able to use the space under the table as well. Inexpensive fold-up tables can be found at discount stores, and you can keep them in your closet until the next party.

Lighting can transform a space—and a face. Everyone looks better in soft lighting. Place candles around the main room and unplug any bright lamps or change to low-watt bulbs. If you have overhead lighting, turn it on low or ideally put it on dimmers, which is an inexpensive option. (See page 14 for more on lighting.)

Flowers are an easy way to beautify a space, and they don't have to be expensive. I like to put two or three bunches of flowers together, keeping the colors separate. Plants are great too; orchids and chile pepper plants have a ton of character and last longer than cut flowers. It's

your party, so follow your instincts. Something as simple as a glass bowl filled with lemons can brighten up a room. Or fill a big bowl with whole walnuts in their shells and add a nutcracker.

Buy some colorful or patterned cocktail napkins at a party store or online. One of my favorite sources for seasonal items is Target (Kmart is great too). Don't think about impressing your guests—think about making them smile! I use paper plates only if absolutely necessary. My father hated plastic dishware and glassware and that feeling has stuck with me—I prefer to drink from a glass and eat from a plate. If you have the storage space, you can buy inexpensive glasses at many different stores, which is usually cheaper than renting them. (See page 5 for more on party rentals.)

Easy Flower Arrangements

✳ **Single-color flower arrangement:**
Buy several bunches of one type of flower in one color, such as white tulips, blue irises, or gerbera daisies. Make sure it's a substantial flower, not a dainty one. Arrange them in any attractive vase, being sure to cut off the ends before adding them to water. (When you mix various colors of the same flower, the arrangement doesn't look quite as elegant.)

✳ **Hydrangeas:** Place four hydrangea plants in a silver punch bowl and cover the stems with moss.

✳ **Herb centerpiece:** Fresh herbs look perfect on a table, and they add a wonderful fragrance. Almost any type of herb will work. Fill low vases with bunches of fresh mint or six small drinking glasses with six different types of herbs (such as mint, rosemary, lavender, flat-leaf parsley, thyme, and oregano). If hot weather makes the herbs look limp, just plunge them in a bowl of ice water and they'll perk right up. Shake to remove excess water.

THE FOOD

Guests always appreciate bite-sized food at cocktail parties, particularly when they're trying to talk, drink, and eat all at once. The fancier the party, the smaller the food. Make it easier on everyone by serving food that is no bigger than two bites. If you don't have time to do anything but heat up frozen pigs in a blanket, no problem. I serve pigs in a blanket at just about every cocktail party I host, and everyone joyfully gobbles them up, especially my husband and my friend Morty. Arrange them on a pretty platter with good mustard and you're halfway there.

Learn to love your oven. Baking is the simplest way to make food quickly. There are countless frozen hors d'œuvres you can buy in just about any supermarket and bake up. Trader Joe's spanakopita and Whole Foods' goat cheese tarts are my favorites. Could I do it from scratch? Sure, and you can do it that way if you enjoy putting in a bit of effort. But you don't need to! The point is to give people tasty treats they enjoy, not to win the chef-of-the-year award. Store-bought hummus will taste no different to most of your friends from hummus you spent an afternoon making at home. Make it easy on yourself so you can relax and have fun. Just be sure to take it out of the package it came in. Presentation is the key—make it look beautiful. I like to write down what food I'm putting out and then match it with a plate, bowl, or platter. Put a sticky note on the tray for each item and you'll be able to have a friend help assemble the trays for you.

Platters are the simplest way to present food on a large scale, but don't panic if you don't have any (see "Platters 101," page 185). Arrange your serving pieces in different areas of your apartment or house so that people move around. Flow is everything, especially in a small space, so give your guests a reason to circulate.

Don't forget to put out a pretty bowl of nuts or a few small bites for people to nibble on while you're getting last-minute details done in the kitchen. I often put out a bowl of apple slices with a squeeze of lemon and a little dipping bowl of honey. Another welcoming sight is a big platter of deviled eggs, especially in these protein-loving times. (Food is particularly important if your guests are driving to and from the party. Don't fill them up with drinks without tasty treats to balance them out.)

Platters 101

The key to arranging platters is choosing the right size. If you're not putting out that much food, use smaller platters and then replenish them; it will make your food seem more plentiful. It's always nice to have a garnish on the platter—use seasonal touches like pinecones, pine branches, holiday ornaments, edible flowers, fresh herbs, and lemons. I often use large leaves to line my platters, especially cheese platters. Banana leaves, lemon leaves, and bamboo leaves are perfect—ask your local florist for a selection. Nowadays you can find reusable fake leaves that are made specifically for food (look for them at craft stores and floral supply stores or at Williams-Sonoma).

If you're putting out dips or spreads on a platter, place the dips in separate containers or bowls and arrange them on the platter, with the bread or veggies laid out separately. The platter looks neater if you don't crowd the food or let it spill over the edges (unless it's something like mini–grilled sandwiches, which look good piled on top of one another), so leave a 1-inch border around the edge of the platter. And if you're going to garnish the platter, do so before you arrange the food around it. If you're garnishing the food on the platter with a sauce (such as a chive oil, balsamic vinegar, or pesto), use a squeeze bottle so that it doesn't spill everywhere.

If you don't own any platters, cover baking sheets with parchment paper and fun garnishes and use those instead. Or use colored paper placemats to cover the bottom. Cutting boards can also double as platters; I love to serve cheeses and all sorts of appetizers on them. But if you do plan to have people over at least a couple of times a year, invest in at least two white platters in two different sizes. I think a long, narrow platter is essential. Platters this size can be used for anything; in addition to entertaining, you can serve dinner on them.

THE DRINKS

At a cocktail party, the drinks are just as important as the food (for some people even more so; those are the ones you have to keep from driving home under the influence!). Red, White, and Bubbly are the way to go. Bubbly is a staple in my pantry, but for parties I stock up as it sets the tone for a festive affair. And lucky for all hosts, there are a variety of options at all price points. My all-time favorite is Domaine Carneros Rose, but when I'm being more budget conscious I choose Cristalino, a great bubbly from Spain. For wines, choose one red and one white; the worst predicament would be running short, so estimate 5 to 6 glasses per bottle.

Creative cocktails set the mood of the party. Drinks like Key Lime Martinis and Kir Royales are easy and fun. Mix up a pitcher of cocktails ahead of time so you can hand the guests a drink when they walk in. Or set up a classic martini bar, with gin, vodka, vermouth, olives, and lemon twists—and a martini shaker, of course. I don't always have a full bar, however. If I'm serving sangría or a specialty cocktail, I may have just wine, beer, and Champagne on hand. (See "Stocking the Bar," page 27.)

I like to put out a silver tray with glasses and a pitcher of water so people can help themselves. If you don't have any pitchers, remove the labels from empty wine bottles and use them to serve water. (People always go to the bar for water, and if they can pour it themselves, it's one less thing for you to do.) You can find inexpensive silver trays at Pottery Barn and at flea markets. No silver tray in your arsenal? Use a colorful plastic tray or a kitschy old flea market tray, or even perhaps a framed mirror. (See "Platters 101," page 185.) Throw a flower on it and you'll be fending off compliments for your creativity.

If you can, hire a bartender to deal with the drinks while you deal with everything else. (A server and a kitchen helper are also nice to have so you're not running around doing everything.) If I'm serving only a couple of hot passed appetizers, my friends are always willing to help. Some people love to pass food and help out; it makes them the belles of the ball. Be sure to ask your most gregarious friend to help you. (For more on wait staff, see "Parties R$_x$," page 6.)

For nondrinkers, put out sparkling juices or sodas in glass bottles along with sparkling water. Or make them a nonalcoholic "cocktail" with fresh lemon juice, mint syrup, a teaspoon of sugar, and club soda with a splash of cranberry juice—there are zillions of concoctions. And don't forget big bowls of lemon and limes with a small cutting board and small serrated knife (a small tomato knife is ideal).

Serving with Attitude: Creative Serving Ideas

One of my signature party foods is a tray of wheatgrass with crudités—people love it because it looks as if the veggies are growing in the grass. It's not necessary to transfer the wheatgrass to a separate container; it usually comes in a nice flat black tray. (You can find wheatgrass at some supermarkets, and any flower shop should be able to order it for you. Buy it up to three days ahead and keep it watered.) I decorate the tray with gerbera daisies secured to bamboo skewers and planted in the grass. You can use flats of grass to cover a table too. To fit the wheatgrass to the table, use a bread knife

or scissors to cut the wheatgrass into strips. Place the strips in galvanized tin flower boxes and arrange them down the table. For another party I placed tulips in the grass to make it look like the flowers were growing there.

When I'm serving a bite-sized appetizer that isn't finger food, like hamachi, caviar, or even mac and cheese, I serve it in spoonfuls on oversize Chinese soupspoons (they're easy to find in Chinatown or online; see Sources). For your carb-conscious friends, use the spoons to serve mini burgers without the buns. Place shredded lettuce on the bottom of the spoon, then add a mini burger patty and a pinch of finely grated cheese and top it with a small piece of tomato. They're also a fun way to serve dessert: make spoonfuls of chocolate mousse, brownie bites, or any kind of pudding with a dab of caramel sauce.

I often serve soup or dessert in little teacups or demitasse cups. They don't have to match—that's what's fun about it. I've also used them to serve risotto, with little espresso spoons instead of forks. Small teacups can be found at Crate & Barrel, or you can rent them.

I've recently discovered bamboo plates and platters, which I use instead of plastic. I like disposable plates from a company called Bambu, but you can find wooden bamboo bowls, plates, and other accessories at many retailers (see Sources). Bamboo cutting boards come in various sizes and also make amazing serving platters.

There are so many fun ways to serve food; these are just some quick thoughts. Take a look around your house and local markets and you'll be able to come up with lots of creative ideas.

Young City Slickers

So you've graduated from college and made it to the big city. You want to show your friends your new pad (even if it's a studio the size of a walk-in closet). What better excuse to throw a party? The party plan can be simple and inexpensive.

The food should be filling and easy to make. Dishes like dips, spreads, and roasted potatoes can be made quickly or purchased at your local market. Toothpick-studded roasted potatoes (cut red potatoes into quarters or use fingerling potatoes) with garlic aïoli dip or blue cheese dip are delicious.

* **Food:** Plan a couple of days ahead and make simple dishes that will fill people up, like hummus with pita bread; veggies like peeled carrot sticks and celery; and snack foods such as pretzels, wasabi peas, or a bag of chips served with a quick sour-cream dip (mix sour cream with Lipton onion soup mix). Or order dumplings from your favorite Chinese restaurant.

    If you're more ambitious, buy salsa, guacamole, sour cream, scallions, chopped black olives, shredded cheese, and canned refried beans and make a seven-layer dip, layering these ingredients from top to bottom on a platter and serving the dip with tortilla chips. Cut pizza into little squares or diamonds to make it more fun. Lay out an easy cheese platter with two types of cheese and grapes. Even frozen taquitos make an easy appetizer.

    Dessert can be as simple as ice pops, ice cream sandwiches, or store-bought mini-cookies. Mochi, a Japanese sticky rice ice cream, is available at many grocery stores and is a tasty twist on ordinary ice cream. Bowls of mini–candy bars and little boxes of Hot Tamales and gumdrops can be served in big bowls. No serving bowls? Buy brown lunch bags, roll them down, and fill them with popcorn and red licorice or your favorite candy.

* **Drinks:** Choose a drink theme and serve one kind of cocktail all night long. You can also tell guests it's BYOB (just be sure to have basics like water, lemons, and soda on hand). I like to make a batch of punch and let guests help themselves. (Try Frozen Lime Punch, page 250.)

* **Music:** Load up the iPod and groove the night away. Or invite your friends to bring CDs they've created from their favorite play lists.

* **Invites:** Just email your friends an invitation to this party. Email sets a casual, come-one, come-all vibe. Or post it on your Facebook or MySpace page or send out an invitation from Pingg.com.

Lulu's Tip

For a fast and easy way to label cheeses or buffet items, use small plastic plant markers (sometimes called *plant labels*, available at garden stores). Just write on them with a sharp pencil or a Sharpie pen and stick them in the cheese or tape them to the side of a serving bowl. I love to serve baskets of crackers and/or breads at my cocktail parties—something crunchy is a great play off a cocktail. Some of my favorite brands of crackers include Carr's Biscuits, Whole Foods 365 brand Wasabi Rice Crackers, and 34° Crispbread Crackers, but try out different brands. It's better to refill a small bowl or basket than use too big a bowl and have it look empty after a few people arrive.

Lulu's Tip

If a food needs to be hot to taste good, don't set it out on a platter, where it will quickly become unappealing. Choose foods that taste good at room temperature, such as veggies and dip or hummus. I hate warmers of any kind unless they're on a formal buffet; warmers are reminiscent of a breakfast buffet. If you're serving appetizers that taste best warm, better to pass them on trays.

Mini Wild Mushroom Risotto Cakes

These earthy, creamy cakes are great for any cocktail party, or you can make bigger cakes using a cookie cutter and serve them as a first course at a dinner party. I keep them in the freezer so that I always have an appetizer on hand. It's also great as a main course served with Escarole and Mesclun Salad with Edamame, Mint, and Pecorino (page 91).

MAKES ABOUT 72 MINI CAKES

4 cups dried or fresh mushrooms, such as porcini, shiitake, and morels

¼ cup extra virgin olive oil

1 cup thinly sliced shallots

2 garlic cloves, minced

6 cups chicken stock

1 cup red wine

2 cups white wine (leftover white wine or Champagne can be used)

2 fresh thyme sprigs or 1 teaspoon dried

1 teaspoon sugar

1 tablespoon kosher salt

2 teaspoons white pepper

½ cup chopped yellow onion

3 cups Arborio rice

8 tablespoons (1 stick) unsalted butter, softened

3 tablespoons dry vermouth

1 cup grated Parmesan, Asiago, or Fontina cheese or a combination

Truffle oil to taste

Crème fraîche

Chopped fresh chives

① Place the dried mushrooms in a bowl of water and soak them overnight. Drain them in a colander.

② In a large saucepan over medium heat, heat 2 tablespoons of the olive oil and add the shallots and garlic. Sauté for 3 to 5 minutes, or until caramelized. If the shallots taste bitter, add a pinch or two of sugar.

③ Add the reconstituted dried or fresh mushrooms, 2 cups of the chicken stock, the red wine, white wine, thyme, sugar, salt, and pepper and bring to a boil over medium heat. Lower the heat and simmer for 10 minutes.

④ Strain the shallot-mushroom mixture through a sieve, reserving the liquid. Remove the sprigs of thyme. Transfer the mixture to the bowl of a food processor and pulse to chop. Set aside.

⑤ Pour the mushroom liquid into a large pot and bring to a boil. Add the remaining 4 cups chicken stock and bring to a boil. Reduce the heat to a simmer and keep it warm.

⑥ To make the risotto, in a large, heavy saucepan, heat the remaining 2 tablespoons olive oil over medium heat and sauté the onion for 4 to 5 minutes. Add the rice and stir for 2 to 3 minutes, until the rice is coated.

7. Increase the heat to medium-high and ladle 2 cups of the stock mixture into the rice. Use a wooden spoon to scrape the bottom of the pot. If you have to walk away from the risotto, cover it completely with liquid. Once the liquid has been absorbed, ladle more broth onto the rice and keep stirring. This will take 20 to 25 minutes total. (If you run out of broth, use hot water. Just pour it in from a kettle on the stove.)

8. About 5 minutes before the risotto is done, add the chopped mushrooms, butter, and vermouth. Stir in the cheese and the truffle oil.

9. Preheat the oven to 400°F. Let the risotto cool by spreading it in a thin layer on a jelly-roll pan. Once the risotto has cooled, form it into little cakes using a tablespoon. Lay the cakes on a baking sheet lined with a Silpat mat or sprayed with nonstick cooking spray.

10. Bake for 8 minutes, flip the cakes over, and bake for another 7 minutes, or just until the outside gets a little crispy. Garnish with crème fraîche and chives.

NOTE: You can also prepare these in advance and flash-freeze them. If you're making these for a dinner party, fill cookie cutters with risotto on a cookie sheet. Pat the risotto down and pull off the cookie cutter. Flash-freeze the shapes, transfer them to a Tupperware container, put it in the freezer, and pull it out the night of the party. The cakes can stay frozen for up to 1 month. Heat them in a 400°F oven for 15 minutes.

Crudités with Lemon-Garlic Aïoli

Crudités and dip are party staples. Choose whatever seasonal veggies you like, but mix up the colors. Some veggies, such as carrots and peppers, can be served raw, while others, like zucchini and asparagus, should be blanched but still have a slight crunch. There's nothing sexy about a limp piece of asparagus! And keep the vegetables separate—it makes it easier to refill the platters.

SERVES 20

FOR THE AÏOLI

1 cup mayonnaise

5 garlic cloves, put through a garlic
  press

Juice of ½ lemon

1 teaspoon sugar

1 teaspoon Tabasco sauce

Salt and freshly ground black pepper
  to taste

FOR THE CRUDITÉS

½ lemon

3 cups button mushrooms, wiped clean
  with a paper towel

One 1-pound bag peeled baby carrots

2 bunches of radishes

2 red bell peppers, sliced

2 yellow bell peppers, sliced

1 bunch of asparagus

1 bag or box of cherry tomatoes

5 green or yellow zucchini

¼ cup chopped fresh herbs (optional)

① Mix all the aïoli ingredients in a large bowl and season to taste. The aïoli will keep for 2 weeks in the refrigerator.

② Rub a little lemon on the mushrooms to prevent them from turning brown.

③ You can make the platter up to a day ahead and store the vegetables in separate Ziploc bags. It's best to blanch the vegetables the morning of the party. (You can blanch the asparagus in boiling water with a teaspoon of baking soda, secured with a rubber band, for 30 seconds. Place the spears in an ice bath and drain—don't leave them in the ice bath or they'll get soggy.) Repeat with the zucchini, blanching it whole, cutting it on an angle to the desired thickness.

④ Arrange the veggies on a platter with a bowl of aïoli and scatter the herbs on top if you like.

Caviar Bar with Blinis

People are always impressed by caviar, but they're even more impressed when it's served with tiny blinis and condiments in a martini glass. Bright orange trout or salmon roe makes an inexpensive and delicious alternative to "traditional" caviar. I love a blini with crème fraîche, onion, and caviar with a squeeze of lemon. I could eat caviar right out of the tin with a spoon—what a treat! Caviar, cupcakes, and Champagne are some of my absolute favorite foods.

MAKES 50 MINI BLINIS

½ cup cornmeal

1 cup potato latke mix

3 or 4 scallions, both white and green
parts, or 6 chives, sliced paper-thin

1½ teaspoons sugar

1 cup milk

¼ teaspoon white pepper

1 teaspoon salt

1 teaspoon finely grated lemon zest

Chopped hard-cooked eggs,
whites and yolks separated

Trout or salmon roe

Crème fraîche

Lemon wedges (optional)

① Mix the cornmeal, latke mix, scallions, sugar, milk, pepper, salt, and lemon zest with ½ cup water. (The batter will look like pancake mix, but let it sit for a minute to thicken.)

② Heat a frying pan over medium heat and spray it with olive oil spray.

③ Pour the batter into a squeeze bottle. Cut off the tip of the bottle and squeeze 1 tablespoon or so of batter into the pan to form a blini about the size of a half-dollar. You may need to shake the squeeze bottle between batches.

④ Cook the blinis as you would pancakes: when you see bubbles form on top of the blini, turn them over (they will take about 2 minutes per side). Repeat with the remaining batter. The blinis don't have to be served hot; they are delicious at room temperature.

⑤ Arrange the eggs, caviar, and crème fraîche in separate martini glasses with small spoons for serving next to a plate of blinis. Serve with lemon wedges if desired.

NOTE: You can make the blinis up to 2 months ahead and freeze them. To freeze, let them cool and layer them in a freezer bag with deli or wax paper between layers. Let frozen blinis thaw on the counter for 15 minutes and reheat in a 400°F oven for 10 minutes. I love to add a little lemon zest to the crème fraîche for extra flavor.

Fennel Seed and Lavender Breadsticks

This is an easy way to use ready-made dough, and these sweet and savory breadsticks are always the first to go at a party. You can use fennel or lavender seeds, but the combination of the two is divine.

MAKES ABOUT 20 BREADSTICKS

½ cup extra virgin olive oil
2 tablespoons sugar
1 tablespoon fennel seeds
1 tablespoon lavender buds (see Note)
1 teaspoon kosher salt

¼ teaspoon ground cumin
One 17-ounce package puff pastry, thawed (I use Pepperidge Farm), or 1 pound frozen pizza dough

① Preheat the oven to 400°F.

② In a bowl, combine the olive oil, sugar, fennel seeds, lavender buds, salt, and cumin.

③ Lightly roll out each 10 × 12-inch sheet of puff pastry on a lightly floured surface. Be sure to flour the rolling pin unless you're using a marble rolling pin. Brush the olive oil mixture over the dough until completely covered.

④ Cut the dough into 2-inch-wide strips and twist each strip into a corkscrew. Be sure to roll them up tight, especially if using puff pastry.

⑤ Lay the breadsticks on an ungreased baking sheet and bake for 12 minutes, or until the breadsticks are nicely browned and crispy. The breadsticks will keep for 5 days in an airtight container.

NOTE: Look for lavender buds at almost any market, online at the Atlantic Spice Company, or at sfherb.com.

JUST AN IDEA: You can make a salad dressing with any leftover olive oil mixture. Add some freshly squeezed lemon juice, salt, and pepper and serve over greens.

Baked Brie with French Bread Crostini

My mother used to make baked Brie with puff pastry for her parties and events, but I make this quick and easy version with crescent rolls. Use any kind of jam you like—raspberry, plum, or even kumquat. Instead of the jam, you can puree fresh grapes and spread the puree on top of the Brie.

SERVES 8

One 8-ounce wheel Brie
1 package Alouette or Boursin cheese, at room temperature, or Lulu's Boursin Cheese (page 41)
½ cup apricot jam

One 44-ounce package refrigerated crescent rolls, one 17-ounce package puff pastry (I use Pepperidge Farm), or 1 frozen premade piecrust, defrosted
1 baguette, thinly sliced

(1) Preheat the oven to 400°F.

(2) Place the Brie in a pie plate or on a jelly-roll pan lined with a Silpat baking mat or sprayed with nonstick cooking spray.

(3) Pat the Alouette cheese on top of the Brie. Spread the jam over the top of the cheese.

(4) Cover the Brie with the dough and bring the ends underneath the cheese so the cheese doesn't ooze out while baking. Cut off any excess dough. (For an extra pretty touch, make a thin rope out of the excess dough and place it in a circle around the Brie. Or make any shapes you like with the dough: flowers, stars, and so on.)

(5) Bake for 20 minutes, or until the crust is golden brown.

(6) Transfer the baked Brie to a serving plate and arrange the bread slices around it. Serve warm.

JUST AN IDEA: You can also make individual Brie puffs by wrapping small chunks of Brie in wonton skins (available in the refrigerated section of most grocery stores) and baking them for 20 minutes at 400°F.

Chicken Skewers with Grape-Cilantro Pesto

I was making chicken salad one day when I realized that grapes and cilantro would make a great salsa served on the side. These skewers are a tasty and healthful version of chicken saté.

SERVES ABOUT 20

1 cup extra virgin olive oil
½ cup freshly squeezed lemon juice
½ cup freshly squeezed lime juice
½ cup orange juice
2 tablespoons Lawry's Seasoned Salt
1 tablespoon white pepper
1 teaspoon ground cumin
½ cup rice wine vinegar

½ cup chopped fresh tarragon
1 teaspoon cayenne
½ cup chopped fresh mint
2 tablespoons grade A or B maple syrup
5 garlic cloves, crushed
3 pounds chicken tenders, thawed if frozen
Grape-Cilantro Pesto (recipe follows)

① To prepare the marinade, combine the olive oil, lemon juice, lime juice, orange juice, seasoned salt, pepper, cumin, vinegar, tarragon, cayenne, mint, maple syrup, and garlic in a large bowl.

② Using a fork, lightly prick the chicken pieces and add them to the marinade. Transfer the chicken and marinade to a Ziploc bag and marinate in the refrigerator for at least 5 hours or overnight.

③ Drain the chicken, reserving the marinade, and pat it dry. Transfer the marinade to a small saucepan and boil it over high heat until reduced by half. Set aside.

④ Soak 1 package of wooden skewers in a bowl of water.

⑤ Heat a grill pan over high heat and spray it with canola oil spray. Cook the chicken in batches until done, about 2 to 3 minutes on each side. (Be careful not to overcook the chicken; the tenders are very thin and cook quickly.) Place the cooked chicken on a jelly-roll pan covered with a wire rack to drain.

⑥ Thread the chicken on the skewers by folding them in half and running the skewer through the middle of the chicken.

⑦ Pour any liquid in the sheet pan into the saucepan with the marinade reduction and stir to combine. Brush the skewers with the marinade.

⑧ Arrange the skewers on a platter and place a bowl of the pesto in the middle for dipping.

NOTE: The skewers don't have to be served hot; they taste just as delish at room temperature. You can make the chicken up to 1 day ahead if you sear them ahead of time and then finish them in the oven.

Grape-Cilantro Pesto

MAKES ABOUT 2 CUPS

1 cup seedless red grapes
1 cup seedless green grapes
1 cup chopped fresh cilantro
1 teaspoon salt

Place the grapes, cilantro, and salt in the bowl of a food processor and pulse until combined.

Dates with Prosciutto and Blue Cheese

This is the best sweet and salty appetizer. I am a huge fan of blue cheese, and the pungent flavor of the cheese with the salty prosciutto and sweet dates makes a decadent combination.

MAKES ABOUT 36 PIECES

One 16-ounce container pitted
   Medjool dates
½ cup blue cheese, softened
8 thin slices (4 ounces) prosciutto,
   cut into thirds

1. Preheat the oven to 400°F.

2. Cut each date in half. Dab 1 teaspoon of blue cheese into each date half, wrap it in ⅓ slice of prosciutto, and place it on a baking sheet. Repeat with the remaining dates.

3. Bake for 1 to 2 minutes, or until the prosciutto is crispy. The dates can be made up to 8 hours ahead. Serve warm or at room temperature.

Lulu's Tip

Substitute fresh figs for the dates when in season. I always pick fresh figs off my neighbors' trees. My friend calls this the "wholesale florist." Substitute goat cheese for the blue cheese and add a drop of balsamic glaze on top of the prosciutto.

Grilled Sweet-and-Spicy Shrimp with Mint-Cilantro Dipping Sauce

This recipe can be used to impress just about anyone. Feel free to change the flavors in this recipe (use more cayenne if you like it superspicy). These shrimp will put a smile on anybody's face—try them!

SERVES 8 AS A MAIN COURSE, 16 AS AN APPETIZER

FOR THE SHRIMP
¼ cup packed golden brown sugar
2 tablespoons freshly squeezed
  lemon juice
2 tablespoons vegetable or canola oil
2 teaspoons lemon zest
½ teaspoon Tabasco sauce
½ teaspoon salt
2 pounds shrimp, peeled and deveined

FOR THE DIPPING SAUCE
2 garlic cloves, peeled
1 cup packed fresh mint leaves
1 cup packed fresh cilantro leaves
1 tablespoon honey or agave nectar
1 teaspoon sesame oil
1 teaspoon salt
2 tablespoons freshly squeezed
  lime juice
½ cup vegetable or canola oil
Dash of Tabasco sauce (optional)

① Mix the sugar, lemon juice, 2 tablespoons of the oil, the lemon zest, Tabasco, and salt together in a medium bowl.

② Add the shrimp and mix to coat. Marinate for at least 30 minutes and up to 8 hours. Remove the shrimp from the refrigerator at least 20 minutes before cooking.

③ While the shrimp is returning to room temperature, make the sauce. Place the garlic in the bowl of a food processor and pulse 5 times. Add the mint, cilantro, honey, sesame oil, salt, lime juice, and canola oil and blend, scraping down the sides occasionally, until the mint and cilantro are finely chopped and the mixture is smooth. (If you don't have a food processor, finely the chop the herbs. Place the herbs, honey, sesame oil, salt, lime juice, and oil in a glass jar with a lid and shake to combine.)

④ Heat a grill or frying pan over medium-high heat. Cook the shrimp for 2 minutes on each side, or until they are pink.

⑤ For a main course, serve the shrimp hot over brown rice with the sauce. The shrimp can also be served at room temperature as an appetizer with the sauce for dipping.

NOTE: Slices of avocado, tomato, and roasted asparagus (sliced diagonally) make nice side dishes to go with the shrimp.

Spinach and Asiago Cheese Sandwiches

Everyone loves grilled cheese, and my secret is potato bread, which tastes richer and is very moist. I've served these everywhere from actor Debi Mazar's baby shower to a Grammy-night bash.

MAKES ABOUT 60 APPETIZER-SIZE SANDWICHES

Truffle oil or chili oil (optional)
½ pound (2 sticks) salted butter, melted
20 slices potato bread
One 12-ounce package 4-cheese blend or grated
  Asiago, Parmesan, fontina, and provolone
3 cups fresh baby spinach or arugula leaves

1. Add a few drops of truffle or chili oil to the melted butter if you want to be fancy.

2. Place a piece of wax paper on each of 2 baking sheets. Spread out 10 pieces of bread on each baking sheet. Using a pastry brush, brush each piece with butter and turn it over.

3. Sprinkle 2 tablespoons cheese on each bread slice and cover loosely with spinach or arugula.

4. Place the other piece of bread on top and butter the top of the bread completely.

5. You can cook the sandwiches in a large frying pan or on a griddle. Spray a frying pan with olive oil spray and bring to medium-high heat. Place 4 or 5 sandwiches in the pan and let them brown for 2 to 3 minutes. Flip them over and cook for 2 to 3 minutes, or until brown. (I press a weight on top of the sandwiches to get them crispy, but you can use a spatula to hold each one down.)

6. To serve, cut off the crusts, then cut each sandwich into 6 bite-sized pieces. Serve warm.

NOTE: If you're not serving the sandwiches that day, cut off the crusts, place the pieces in a freezer bag, separating the layers with deli paper. To reheat frozen sandwiches, place them on a baking sheet and bake them in a 375°F oven for 10 minutes. They will keep for up to 1 month in the freezer. These are delicious right out of the oven brushed with white balsamic vinegar or a little bit of truffle oil.

Mini Double-Stuffed New Potatoes

My friend Marcy always used to make double-stuffed potatoes when we were roommates in New York City. Your guests will love these old-school treats. You can also serve them for dinner alongside grilled steak. I always add a little truffle oil to the crème fraîche.

MAKES 30 POTATO HALVES

15 baby red or creamer potatoes, scrubbed
1 tablespoon extra virgin olive oil
¼ cup crème fraîche
½ cup Lulu's Boursin Cheese (page 41)

½ teaspoon salt
½ teaspoon white pepper
3 scallions, both white and green parts, thinly sliced
5 strips Maple-Glazed Bacon, crumbled (page 44)

1. Preheat the oven to 450°F.

2. Cut the potatoes in half crosswise. Using a melon baller, scoop out the center of each potato. Place the insides of the potatoes on a sheet pan. Toss with the olive oil.

3. Bake the potatoes until just tender, 20 to 25 minutes, and let cool completely.

4. Place the potato bits in a mixing bowl. (If the potatoes do not stand upright, slice off a thin portion of the bottoms.)

5. Add the crème fraîche, cheese, salt, and pepper and mash with a fork until creamy.

6. Spoon a small amount into each potato. (This is easier with a pastry bag.) Garnish with the scallions and crumbled bacon.

NOTE: The potatoes can be reheated in the oven 5 minutes before serving, but they're just as delicious at room temperature.

Caramel-Fudge Brownies

My younger sisters used to make these brownies at least twice a week in the summer. They're great frozen—just pop them in your mouth. This is a simple recipe that you can make with your kids or kids can make with their friends. One bite will make your eyes grow wide.

MAKES 36 SMALL BROWNIES

One 18-ounce box Duncan Hines Moist Deluxe devil's food cake mix
⅔ cup milk
8 tablespoons (1 stick) unsalted butter or margarine, melted
1 cup caramel dip or 25 Kraft caramels (see Note)
6 ounces semisweet chocolate chips

① Preheat the oven to 350°F. Grease a 9 x 13-inch baking pan.

② Combine the cake mix, ⅓ cup of the milk, and the melted butter to form a dough in a large bowl. Press half the dough into the pan.

③ Bake for 6 minutes.

④ In a double boiler, melt the caramel with the remaining ⅓ cup milk. Stir with a wooden spoon until smooth.

⑤ Sprinkle the chocolate chips evenly over the brownie base. Top with melted caramel, spreading it as evenly as possible over the layer of chocolate chips.

6. Using your fingers or a large spoon, flatten the remaining brownie mixture in even globs on top of the caramel layer. (Wearing a pair of disposable latex gloves makes this easier.)

7. Bake for 18 minutes more, then set the pan aside to cool. Place the pan, uncovered, in the freezer for 1 hour.

8. Remove and cut into squares (they're easier to cut when they're frozen). I keep the brownies in the freezer in a Ziploc bag, letting them come to room temperature before serving. (Or eat them frozen!)

NOTE: You can find caramel dip in the produce section of most supermarkets.

Key Lime Martini

When I was little, I used to fill a Dixie cup with water and swirl a Dum-Dum lollipop in it, and that inspired my "Lulu twist" of garnishing this sweet and tart drink with a Jolly Rancher lollipop.

SERVES 4

1 cup pineapple juice
3 tablespoons Torani brand vanilla syrup
3 tablespoons sweet and sour mix
Juice of 1 lime
1 cup vodka
Jolly Rancher lollipops

Shake the pineapple juice, syrup, sweet and sour mix, lime juice, and vodka in a cocktail shaker filled with ice. Serve in martini glasses, garnished with a lollipop.

"SHAKEN, NOT STIRRED": A GUYS-ONLY DINNER

Load the DVD player with James Bond movies, invite those tough guys over, and settle in for a guys-only bash. When my husband invites his friends over for dinner and cigars, I make his favorite foods: steak, mashed potatoes, and my mother's famous chocolate cake, which he always asks for. I call it the "Salute to Men" night, which could mean husbands, brothers, boyfriends, or significant others—any and all of your favorite guys.

The food is hearty and guy-friendly, with pasta, meat, and some tasty appetizers. Guys love a baked potato bar where they can customize their potato. Choose from the recipe list and customize it to your guy's tastes. That goes for drinks too; stock up on their favorite beers and/or wines. After dinner, set out a tray with glasses of cognac, Scotch, Sambuca, or a favorite after-dinner drink along with cigars.

DÉCOR

The idea is to create an old-fashioned men's club atmosphere, with classic cocktails and fantastic food. The 21 Club in New York City has a classic men's club ambience, with white tablecloths and an old wooden bar. But I also think of Ralph Lauren, with a fire roaring and the men dressed in dapper outfits sitting in leather chairs with tartan blankets—these are the feelings you want to evoke. For this party, set a masculine table: a dark tablecloth, cool ashtrays placed down the table, and if you really want to score points, find an antique rifle and buckshot and use it as decoration.

Use the DVD player as video art—play the James Bond films with no sound and tune the stereo or iPod to "Rat Pack" tunes. If the guys are sports fanatics, tune in to a sports channel or play DVDs of past games or sports highlights.

A Guide to Manly Drinks

Some evenings you just want to break out the good stuff—and for guys that usually means old-fashioned spirits. But if you can't tell a bottle of cognac from a bottle of Scotch, here's a primer to get you started so you buy the right stuff. If you're really uncertain, ask someone at a good wine and spirits store. (And remember, always keep a bottle of port on hand.)

✻ **Whisky:** Whisky and whiskey are the same thing; the Scots and the Canadians drop the e, but they are all grain-based alcohols. Made in Scotland, Ireland, Canada, and the United States, they differ depending on what grain is used, how it's processed, and how it's blended and aged.

Scotch whisky comes in three varieties: single malt, vatted malt, and blended Scotch. Glenfiddich and Laphroaig are some of the best and most popular brands of single-malt whisky. Single-malt is considered the best but only small amounts are produced. Bourbon is the most well-known American whiskey and is made from at least 51 percent corn. Some of the most popular bourbons include Knob Creek, Maker's Mark, Wild Turkey, and Jim Beam. Rye whiskey is made only in America and is not blended; Jim Beam and Seagram's 7 Crown are two of the bigger brands. Irish whiskey has a stronger flavor than Scottish or American whiskys; Bushmills is a commonly found brand. Canadian whisky is made from corn, barley, and other grains. Some of the most famous brands include Black Velvet, Canadian Club, and McGuiness.

Single-malt Scotch is almost always served straight up, with a few drops of water, while some serve it in large snifters. Blended Scotch and American whiskys are served on the rocks and often used as a mixer in cocktails. Irish whisky is traditionally diluted with water or served neat.

✻ **Cognac:** This is a French spirit, pronounced CONE-yak, that has been made in the Cognac region in western France since the twelfth century. Cognac is produced by distilling white wine after fermentation. The final product contains about 72 percent alcohol. There are three main aging categories that will be indicated on the label (although most producers admit that the designations have more to do with marketing than the quality of the stuff in the bottle). Martell, Hennessy, Courvoisier, and Remy-Martin are the best-known Cognac producers. What sets each brand apart is their secret formula. Some top smaller producers to look for are Delamin, Frapin, and Hine. A good bottle of Cognac will set you back about $100, but you can find decent examples starting around $30.

Cognac is traditionally served as an after-dinner drink to help ease the pain of a big meal, and its full aromas are best when served around 66°F in tulip-shaped glasses.

* **Sambuca:** Sambuca is a well-known Italian liqueur that tastes like black licorice. Serve Sambuca neat as an after-dinner drink, with coffee beans floating on top. Sambuca happens to be my husband's favorite after-dinner drink, along with a cigar.

The Stevie D (Pineapple Juice and Vodka)

This drink is my husband's concoction. He prefers it a little lighter on the vodka.

SERVES 1

1 part pineapple juice
1 part vodka

Combine the juice and vodka in a cocktail shaker filled with ice. Serve in a martini glass.

Dirty Martini

Until recently I thought dirty martinis were a guys' drink. I tried one when I reunited with my childhood friend Beth Arrowood over a sushi dinner. Now I am hooked.

SERVES 1

2 ounces potato vodka or another favorite vodka
1 tablespoon dry vermouth
2 tablespoons olive juice
3 olives

Put the vodka, vermouth, and olive juice in a shaker filled with ice and shake. Serve straight up in a martini glass and garnish with 3 olives: one for health, one for wealth, and one for happiness.

Sidecar

There are numerous stories about the origins of the sidecar, but Harry's Bar in Paris is generally credited with inventing it in the early 1900s for a patron who often rode in the sidecar of a motorcycle. I am grateful to my friend CZ, aka Christina Zilbur, who reintroduced me to the sidecar. CZ prefers her sidecar with a sugared rim.

SERVES 1

1 1/2 ounces brandy
1/2 ounce Triple Sec
1/2 ounce freshly squeezed lemon or lime juice

Combine all the ingredients in a shaker filled with ice, shake well, and strain into a cocktail glass.

Whiskey Sour

SERVES 1

1½ ounces bourbon
1½ ounces freshly squeezed lemon juice
¾ ounce Basic Simple Syrup (page 58)
1 maraschino cherry

Shake the bourbon, lemon juice, and simple syrup in a cocktail shaker filled with ice. Strain into a chilled cocktail glass and garnish with a cherry.

Cigar Primer

Some men (and women) love nothing more than puffing on a cigar. If you're not a cigar aficionado yourself, this primer can help you choose one for your guests (or the cigar lover in your life).

Cigars come in various sizes and colors. The size is determined by the ring size or circumference (one ring is $1/64$ of an inch). The larger the ring size, the more complex the flavor. Color indicates the intensity of the cigar; the darker the wrapper, the more intense the flavor. The colors range from Claro (light tan), Colorado (reddish dark brown), and Natural (light brown) to Colorado Claro (midbrown), Colorado Maduro (dark brown), Maduro (darkest brown), and Oscuro or Double Maduro (black). When checking for freshness, make sure the cigar is spongy or squishy but springs back to the touch. Conversely, it shouldn't be too dry or fragile. The wrapper, filler, and region all affect flavor.

At good tobacco shops, you won't have to buy a whole box of cigars—you can buy them individually—and prices range from $7 to $25 each. According to my cigar-loving husband, if you're choosing cigars for new smokers, Coronas and Robustos are the best choice, and seasoned cigar smokers will know what they want.

I like to put Dunhill mini cigars out in a silver bowl or even More brand brown cigarettes. Go to a smoke shop and see what they suggest. It creates a great visual effect, particularly with a couple of unusual lighters and some matches.

Basic Marinade

MAKES 1 CUP

½ cup port
½ cup balsamic vinegar
Splash of red wine (optional)
Salt and pepper (optional)

Bring the mixture to a boil and reduce the heat to simmer for 5 minutes. Remove from the heat, cool, and use to marinate salmon or steak or serve hot over steak. (To make the marinade into a sauce, add a splash of red wine along with salt and pepper.)

Lulu's Tip

Marinades give everything so much more flavor. You can start to marinate the night before or a few hours ahead. (Just don't marinate fish for more than two hours or the acid will start to cook the fish.) If you have absolutely no time to marinate, brush the marinade on the meat or fish while you're cooking it and reserve a few spoonfuls to brush on the cooked food. (To avoid contamination, any marinade that's touched meat should be brought to a boil before it's used again on the cooked food.)

Lulu's Marvelous Marinade

This is my go-to marinade. It's great for almost anything grilled, especially steak or chicken. Reduce any leftover marinade and use it as an extra sauce to serve on the side.

MAKES 1 ½ CUPS

1 cup hoisin sauce
¾ cup freshly squeezed lime juice
5 garlic cloves, crushed
1 teaspoon hot red pepper flakes
1 tablespoon freshly ground espresso
  beans

2 tablespoons Asian fish sauce
  (nam pla)
½ cup chopped fresh cilantro

Combine all the ingredients and stir briefly to blend. Taste the mixture. If it's too strongly flavored (which it may be, especially if your hoisin sauce is strong), add water, 1 teaspoon at a time, until the flavor mellows.

Maui Onion Dip

This is a great dip for wings, potato chips, pretzels, or even spread on a roast beef sandwich. It also makes a tasty pasta sauce.

MAKES 1 ½ CUPS

3 tablespoons extra virgin olive oil
4 shallots, roughly chopped
1 Maui onion, roughly chopped
¼ cup port
¼ cup balsamic vinegar
2 tablespoons packed brown sugar
1½ cups crumbled blue cheese

¾ cup mayonnaise or cream cheese
¾ cup sour cream
1½ teaspoons pepper
2 teaspoons salt
¼ cup finely chopped fresh chives
Tabasco (optional)

① Heat the olive oil in a large saucepan over medium heat and add the shallots and onion. Sauté for 5 minutes, or until the onion is translucent.

② Add the port, vinegar, and brown sugar and bring to a boil. Reduce the heat and simmer for 3 minutes, stirring constantly. Remove from the heat to cool slightly.

③ Pour the mixture into the bowl of a food processor or blender and add the blue cheese, mayonnaise or cream cheese, sour cream, pepper, and salt. Process or blend until smooth and stir in the chives and Tabasco if desired.

JUST AN IDEA: You can easily turn this dip into a salad dressing by adding ½ cup olive oil, ½ cup champagne vinegar, and salt and pepper. Whisk to combine.

Homemade Hummus with Pita Chips

MAKES 2 CUPS HUMMUS AND 64 PITA CHIPS

FOR THE HUMMUS

Two 15-ounce cans chickpeas, drained
 and rinsed

1 garlic clove, peeled

1 teaspoon ground cumin

⅛ teaspoon cayenne

¼ cup freshly squeezed lemon juice

1 teaspoon grated lemon zest

2 teaspoons salt

¼ teaspoon white pepper

½ teaspoon sesame oil

1 teaspoon honey or agave nectar

¼ cup extra virgin olive oil, plus oil for
 serving

Chopped fresh cilantro (optional)

Paprika (optional)

FOR THE PITA CHIPS

8 pita breads

4 tablespoons (½ stick) salted butter,
 melted, or ¼ cup olive oil

1 teaspoon garlic salt

① For the hummus, puree the chickpeas, garlic, cumin, cayenne, lemon juice, zest, salt, pepper, sesame oil, honey, ¼ cup olive oil, and ⅛ cup hot water together in a food processor until smooth.

② Drizzle with extra virgin olive oil and garnish with cilantro and paprika if desired. Serve with pita chips. The hummus will keep for up to 1 week in the fridge.

③ For the pita chips, cut around the edge of each piece of pita bread and then cut each round into 4 wedges. Separate the wedges so that you get 8 pita wedges from each piece of pita bread.

④ To make the garlic butter, combine the butter and garlic salt in a small bowl.

⑤ Place the pitas wedges rough side up on a baking sheet. Brush with the garlic butter.

⑥ Place the baking sheet under a broiler until the pita chips are done to your satisfaction. Don't walk away from the broiler or they'll burn! The chips will keep in a Tupperware container for 1 week.

Lahmajoons (Armenian Pizza)

My husband's Armenian grandmother and mother used to make lahmajoons for him, and they're his favorites. His grandmother Sirphue and mother Wheezy make their own dough, but I find tortillas to be an easy and delicious shortcut. Lamb adds a nice richness to the pizzas, but you could easily use chicken or beef. They make a great main course, served with a big green salad with a light dressing alongside, and the miniature versions make terrific party appetizers.

MAKES 18 PIZZAS (TO SERVE 8 TO 10 AS A MAIN COURSE) OR 54 APPETIZER-SIZE LAHMAJOONS

3 pounds ground lamb or ground chicken or beef
2 onions, finely chopped
3 green bell peppers, finely chopped
10 garlic cloves, minced
2 cups chopped fresh flat-leaf parsley
3 cups chopped fresh mint
2 cups chopped fresh cilantro
One 6-ounce can tomato paste
One 24-ounce jar marinara sauce (I like Silver Palate, Newman's Own, and Prego brands)

2 tablespoons Lawry's Seasoned Salt
1 tablespoon white or black pepper
2 teaspoons hot red pepper flakes
Juice of 2 lemons, plus 6 to 8 lemons cut into wedges for serving
2 tablespoons sugar
Three 33-ounce packages 5- or 6-inch flour or corn tortillas

① Preheat the oven to 400°F.

② Place the lamb in a large bowl. Add the onions, bell peppers, garlic, herbs, tomato paste, marinara sauce, salt, pepper, hot pepper flakes, lemon juice, and sugar and combine with your hands—really work it through with your hands.

③ Make a small patty and cook it in a frying pan to test for seasoning, adding more Lawry's Seasoned Salt to taste.

④ Lay out the tortillas on a baking sheet. You can use them whole or cut them in half (and more will fit on the baking sheet). For the mini lahmajoons, use a 2-inch cookie cutter and cut out tortilla circles (you'll get 3 circles per tortilla; fry up any tortilla scraps in oil and make tortilla strips to use as garnish for salad or as croutons).

⑤ Using your hands, spread the lamb mixture on the tortilla all the way to the edges, patting it down. The mixture should be spread thinly, but thick enough so that the tortilla isn't visible.

6. Bake for 15 to 20 minutes, or until golden brown. The mini lahmajoons don't have to be served hot—they're just as good at room temperature. Serve with a bowl of lemon wedges to squeeze over the top.

NOTE: If you're making the pizzas earlier in the day, bake for 15 minutes and then reheat for 5 to 10 minutes at 350°F. You can also freeze the lahmajoons by layering them with deli paper or tinfoil and placing them in a Tupperware container for up to a month. Reheat in a preheated 350°F oven for 10 minutes.

JUST AN IDEA: You could serve toppings with the pizzas for a dinner party so that people can garnish their own. Stevie's favorite garnish is sliced peperoncini and on the side I serve a platter of sliced tomatoes, avocados, onions drizzled with olive oil, and balsamic vinegar. I also like to make a green salad with balsamic vinaigrette, layer it on top of a lahmajoon, fold it in half, and eat it like a taco.

Port-Marinated Beef Filet

The port marinade in this recipe can be used on fish and chicken as well. For best results, marinate your meat overnight. Serve with your guy's favorite vegetable.

SERVES 8

½ cup port

½ cup soy sauce

½ cup balsamic vinegar

½ cup packed brown sugar

1 tablespoon fennel seeds

1 teaspoon hot red pepper flakes

1 teaspoon Lawry's Seasoned Salt

1 teaspoon white pepper

1 tablespoon fresh rosemary leaves

5 garlic cloves, put through a press

Eight 6-ounce filet mignons

1. Combine the port, soy sauce, vinegar, brown sugar, fennel seeds, red pepper flakes, seasoned salt, white pepper, rosemary, and garlic in a saucepan.

2. Bring to a boil over medium-high heat and simmer for 5 minutes. Let cool.

3. Tenderize the meat with a fork and place it in 2 Ziploc bags or a plastic storage container. Add the marinade, seal the bags or container, and marinate for at least 1 hour and up to 8 hours or overnight in the refrigerator. Pull the meat out of the refrigerator 1 hour before cooking (less if it's a very hot day).

4. When you're ready to cook, remove the meat and reserve the marinade.

5. Heat a pan on high and sear each filet or grill for 4 minutes per side. (The meat will keep cooking once you remove it from the pan.)

6. Let the meat rest for 10 minutes before serving. If you want to cook the meat before guests arrive, sear it for 3 minutes per side and reheat it in a 425°F oven for 10 minutes.

7. You can serve the reserved marinade as a sauce on the meat if you boil it for several minutes first.

Lulu's Tip

For overcooked steak, combine 1 cup of beef broth, 1 cup of red wine, and a pinch of brown sugar in a saucepan. Add your favorite dried herbs and a pinch of hot red pepper flakes and boil for 10 minutes. Strain and pour into a gravy boat, pouring some over the steak to make it juicy.

Wasabi and Leek Potato Mash

I learned about wasabi after college, when I ate at my first sushi restaurant in New York City. In my repertoire of mashed potatoes, the wasabi mash is my favorite, but you can easily come up with your own creations. I love adding grated Parmesan cheese to plain mashed potatoes, but add your favorite cheese, fresh herbs, or sautéed mushrooms.

SERVES 8 AS A SIDE DISH

2 pounds potatoes, such as Idaho or russet, peeled and cut into quarters

2 tablespoons chicken or vegetable Better Than Bouillon or one 15-ounce can chicken or vegetable stock

1 tablespoon extra virgin olive oil

1 tablespoon packed brown sugar

2 leeks, thinly sliced

4 shallots, thinly sliced

4 garlic cloves, thinly sliced

8 tablespoons (1 stick) unsalted butter

1 tablespoon wasabi powder

¾ cup heavy cream or whole milk, warmed gently, or more if desired

Salt and white pepper to taste

① Place the potatoes in a large pot and cover them with water. Add the bouillon, bring to a boil, and simmer for 30 minutes. (If you're using stock, put it in before the water and add water to cover the potatoes.) Do not overcook or poke them too often to check doneness, or they'll absorb too much broth.

② While the potatoes are boiling, heat the olive oil in a sauté pan over medium heat and add the brown sugar, leeks, shallots, and garlic. Sauté for about 10 minutes.

③ When the potatoes are done, drain them in a colander and then mash them well with a potato masher or put them through a food mill.

④ Return them to the pot over very low heat and stir in the butter.

⑤ In a small bowl, mix the wasabi powder with 1 teaspoon water. Gradually add the cream, wasabi, and shallot mixture to the mashed potatoes, beating with a wooden spoon until the potatoes reach the desired smoothness. Add more cream or milk to taste. If you're not going to serve them immediately, add extra cream or milk to keep them creamy.

⑥ To keep warm for up to an hour, place them in a baking dish wrapped in aluminum foil, turning the oven to 200°F. Or reheat in a microwave.

NOTE: You can make the potatoes a day ahead and reheat them in the microwave with milk or cream (to taste) or place them in a pan over low heat and stir constantly. To freeze them, transfer to a freezer container and freeze for up to 1 month. Reheat by defrosting in the microwave or over the stove.

Tomato-Brie Penne

Men love pasta, and this is my go-to recipe. My favorite way to prepare this dish is to marinate all the ingredients (except the pasta) in a bowl overnight in the refrigerator so that the flavors really come together.

SERVES 4 TO 6

1 pound penne pasta

2 quarts chicken stock (optional)

1½ pounds ripe Brie, rind removed and cheese cut into chunks

6 to 8 Roma or plum tomatoes, chopped, or one 28-ounce can chopped tomatoes, drained

4 garlic cloves, minced

1 cup julienned fresh basil leaves, plus whole basil leaves for garnish

¼ cup extra virgin olive oil

1 teaspoon sugar

½ teaspoon hot red pepper flakes

Lawry's Seasoned Salt to taste

Freshly ground black pepper to taste

1. Cook the pasta in a large pot of salted boiling water for 6 to 8 minutes, or until al dente. I boil the pasta in chicken stock to give it more flavor.

2. As the pasta cooks, mix the Brie, tomatoes, garlic, basil, extra virgin olive oil, and sugar together in a large bowl.

3. Drain the pasta and add it to the tomato and Brie mixture, stirring until the cheese is melted. If you used chicken stock to cook the pasta, add ½ cup to help melt the cheese and blend the seasonings.

4. Add the red pepper flakes, seasoned salt, and pepper to taste and continue to toss. Adjust the seasonings to your liking.

5. Garnish with whole basil leaves and serve hot.

Patty P's Chocolate Cake

My mother is known from Maine to Malibu for this cake. It is decadent. You can make it ahead of time and freeze it unglazed. I julienned roses to garnish the top and sides.

MAKES ONE 10-INCH CAKE; SERVES 10 TO 12

FOR THE CAKE

½ cup semisweet chocolate chips or
  4 ounces semisweet chocolate
2 tablespoons unsweetened cocoa
  powder
1 teaspoon ground cinnamon
2¼ cups granulated sugar
4 large eggs
¾ pound (3 sticks) salted butter, at
  room temperature
1 cup sour cream
2 tablespoons dark rum
¾ cup plus 2 tablespoons cake flour

2 teaspoons baking powder
1 teaspoon baking soda
1 teaspoon salt

FOR THE GLAZE

3/4 cup semisweet chocolate chips or
  6 ounces semisweet chocolate
½ cup confectioners' sugar, sifted
Pinch of salt
4 tablespoons (½ stick) unsalted butter,
  at room temperature
2 teaspoons dark rum

① Preheat the oven to 325°F. Spray a 10-inch round springform pan with baking spray. Line the bottom of the pan with parchment paper and spray the parchment with baking spray.

② Put the chocolate, cocoa, cinnamon, and ½ cup of the granulated sugar in the bowl of a food processor and process until the chocolate has been finely incorporated. Add ⅔ cup of boiling water through the feed tube and then add the eggs one at a time, processing after each addition. Add the remaining 1¾ cups sugar, the butter, sour cream, and rum and combine.

③ In a large bowl, mix the flour, baking powder, baking soda, and salt together. Pour the flour mixture into the food processor and pulse to combine. Do not overprocess.

④ Pour the cake batter into the prepared cake pan. Bake for 1½ hours, or until a toothpick inserted into the middle of the cake comes out clean, checking the cake after 50 minutes.

⑤ To make the glaze, combine the chocolate chips, ¼ cup water, the confectioners' sugar, and the salt in a double boiler over boiling water, stirring constantly until there are no lumps. Add the butter and remove from the heat. Stir in the rum.

⑥ Remove the cake from the oven and let it cool in the pan for at least 1 hour. Gently place the cake on a serving platter or cake round and spread the glaze on top using an offset spatula.

DINNER PARTY ON THE FLY

The doorbell rings. It's your best friend and her husband, who were just "in the neighborhood." And it's dinnertime. Instead of calling for take-out pizza for the second time this week, hand them a drink and disappear to the pantry, where you can create an impromptu dinner in no time flat.

My house is like Grand Central Station, and especially at dinnertime I have to be ready for unexpected guests. I always act as if it's no problem when they arrive. The trick is to be prepared. One night I was planning to go to bed early and I didn't realize that Stevie had told our friend to stop by. I leapt out of bed, put out a bowl of nuts, and opened a bottle of Pinot Noir. Then I ran to the kitchen and pulled out flour tortillas, tomato sauce, and goat cheese. I made simple pizzas by adding fresh basil and grilled them in my oven. They were a hit—we ended up going through an entire pack of tortillas that night. I served cookies for dessert, because I happened to have frozen cookie dough in the freezer. This was my Party Pantry at work (see page 22): I had the ingredients on hand and a bottle of wine, and frankly there wasn't much more I could have made because my refrigerator was empty.

These recipes are easy to pull together in just a few minutes. The hot chocolate pudding is especially easy: I love using the MarieBelle brand of hot chocolate to make a quick pudding. If you can't get it, make a quick and tasty dessert using chocolate wafers layered with whipped cream.

CREATING A PARTY FROM A CONVENIENCE STORE

Convenience stores such as 7-Eleven, Wawa, and corner delis have it all, from coffee, ice cream, and nuts to crackers, candy, cookies, and flowers. From specialty beers like Red Stripe to an impressive selection of wines, sparkling wines, and liquor, you can probably find it at your local convenience store. Once again, make the store-bought food your own; add some chopped herbs or a dash of Tabasco to take it up a notch.

If you're really in a pinch, you can always head to the corner market and throw a "grazing" (see page 180): buy cheese (if available), crackers, nuts, frozen pizza, or frozen burritos, make some cocktails, and call it a night. You can buy dessert too. Who wouldn't be psyched to dig into a plate of Hostess cupcakes, powdered sugar or chocolate Donettes, or Twinkies for dessert?

COOKING FROM THE PANTRY: LULU'S FAVORITE DISHES

Using the Party Pantry list on page 22, you can make many fun dishes and last-minute party spreads. (Of course, this all depends on what's in your refrigerator. The more fresh ingredients you have, the more recipes you can create.) Dips are easy to make with mayonnaise or sour cream, garlic salt, Tabasco, and dill. If you have goat cheese or yogurt, mix it with harissa (see Sources) for a fiery dip (harissa is also great mixed with mayonnaise). Out of crackers? Cut tortillas into triangles and bake them until crisp. Instant risotto is a lifesaver: make a bowl of risotto or prepare Mini Wild Mushroom Risotto Cakes (page 190). You can make Mexican hot chocolate for dessert, with marshmallows to garnish, or dip store-bought shortbread cookies in melted chocolate. Make instant s'mores in a pinch: cut graham crackers in half, layer them with chocolate and marshmallows, and stick them under the broiler (see page 144).

Quick and Easy Pasta Dishes

There's nothing faster than pasta. Using just penne, you can create a million different pasta dishes and serve them cold or hot. If you have cheese in your freezer, pasta in the pantry, and butter in the fridge, you can do anything.

For a fast hot pasta dish, just throw canned artichokes, minced fresh garlic or garlic salt, olive oil, lemon juice, salt, pepper, and diced canned tomatoes into a saucepan and heat on low. I also love to add mashed anchovies to almost any pasta dish.

If you have garlic butter in the freezer, pull it out and toss it with spaghetti and some hot red pepper flakes. Throw in any fresh or leftover veggies you have. (Just chop up raw veggies and cook them in the pasta water.) Don't be scared—be creative! If you keep jarred pasta sauce in your pantry, you've got an instant spaghetti dish. And remember that pasta can be an appetizer or an amuse-bouche: just serve it in little bowls or cups with small spoons for a fun cocktail bite.

MY GO-TO INGREDIENTS

There are a few things I can't cook without: maple syrup, truffle salt, lemon and/or lime juice, garlic, Tabasco, and balsamic demi-glace. You can instantly transform a dish with these simple ingredients, or just give a little needed flavor boost.

✳ Maple syrup can be used to flavor almost everything, but it's especially useful to counteract salt in a dish. Maple syrup will caramelize on and sweeten a piece of fish. I add it to almost every marinade and use it in my tea as a natural sweetener.

✳ Truffle salt is absolutely one of my favorites, and I love introducing it to people. I adore the flavor of truffles, but fresh truffles are expensive and hard to find. Truffle salt is the next best thing. I sprinkle it on everything, even frozen pizza.

✳ If I feel there's something missing from a soup, I add a little lemon or lime juice and a hit of Tabasco, and it always seems to work. I never used or cooked with Tabasco until I met my husband, whose whole family puts it on everything. (My favorite treat is a hot dog with sweet potato fries and a side of mayonnaise mixed with Tabasco for dipping.) It adds a kick to everything—I love it!

✳ I could eat garlic all day long. Even when I'm sick, I eat raw garlic and olive oil on bread. If something needs a kick and you're not sure what it needs (and you haven't already added garlic), add 1 clove of chopped garlic or more until you like the flavor. To roast garlic, wrap it in aluminum foil and bake it in a 375°F oven for about 50 minutes, or until the garlic is soft. Remove the roasted head of garlic from the foil, place it in a ramekin, and cover the garlic halfway with chicken stock. Sprinkle blue cheese over the top and bake for 10 minutes. Squeeze the roasted garlic and cheese into the ramekin and use it as a dip for bread.

✳ Balsamic glaze is so versatile, whether you serve it over sliced tomatoes and mozzarella or on a fresh avocado, quesadillas, or pizza. Drizzling it over Brussels sprouts gives them a deep flavor, and it transforms a salad dressing. The best part is, it's simple to make. Just reduce balsamic vinegar to a syrup in a small, heavy pan over low heat, and it takes on a whole new flavor—there's no tang to it, just a rich sweetness. (If you've ever tasted a really expensive aged balsamic vinegar, you'll know what I'm talking about.) I make my own and keep it in the refrigerator, but you can buy it at some specialty stores.

Lulu's Luscious Mixed Nuts

I started making these when my friend Jennifer Feinstein still sold her own brand of "Just Not Crazy . . . Nuts." This blend of spices may sound odd, but it creates a wonderful combination of savory and sweet and will last for weeks in your pantry. I like to keep the nuts in a glass jar with a scoop for unexpected guests or wrap up a jar and give them as a gift. Serving these homemade nuts is ten steps above putting out a bowl of ordinary roasted nuts.

SERVES ABOUT 20

5 cups assorted nuts, such as walnuts, almonds, hazelnuts, cashews, pecans, and pumpkin seeds
3 tablespoons butter
4 tablespoons packed brown sugar
2 tablespoons honey or agave nectar

¼ teaspoon cayenne
2 teaspoons Lawry's Seasoned Salt
1 teaspoon white pepper
2 teaspoons curry powder
3 tablespoons chopped fresh rosemary

① Preheat the oven to 400°F.

② Place the nuts on a jelly-roll pan and bake for 10 minutes.

③ Transfer the roasted nuts to a large mixing bowl.

④ Place the remaining ingredients (except 1 tablespoon of the brown sugar and 1 tablespoon of the rosemary) in a large sauté pan and cook over low heat until the butter is melted, stirring constantly.

⑤ Pour the spiced melted butter over the roasted nuts and mix well.

⑥ Pour the nuts back onto the baking sheet and bake for 15 to 18 minutes, or until golden brown.

⑦ Sprinkle the remaining 1 tablespoon brown sugar and 1 tablespoon rosemary on the nuts and serve.

NOTE: The nuts will keep in an airtight container for up to 2 weeks (just let them cool before transferring them to the container).

Spaghetti with Ten-Minute Tomato Sauce

Anybody can make this dish. For an adult version, add a splash of vodka to the sauce.

SERVES 6

½ cup extra virgin olive oil

2 cups diced onion

8 garlic cloves, sliced

Two 28-ounce cans diced tomatoes

One 12-ounce jar roasted red peppers
  or sun-dried tomatoes

1 teaspoon hot red pepper flakes

1 teaspoon sugar

½ cup thinly sliced fresh basil leaves
  or 2 teaspoons dried

1 cup heavy cream (optional)

1 pound penne or spaghetti

① Heat the olive oil in a large sauté pan over medium-high heat. Add the onion and garlic and sauté for about 3 minutes, or until the onion is translucent. Add the tomatoes, red peppers or sun-dried tomatoes, red pepper flakes, and sugar and bring to a boil.

② Reduce the heat to low and add the basil. Stir in the heavy cream if desired.

③ Meanwhile, cook the pasta according to the package directions.

④ Toss the cooked pasta with the tomato sauce and serve.

JUST AN IDEA: I love to cook my pasta in chicken broth instead of water; it adds more flavor.

Lulu's Tip

If you want to add veggies to a pasta dish, add them to the pasta water while the pasta is cooking. Alternatively, add the veggies to the tomato sauce and let them cook until soft.

MarieBelle Hot Chocolate Pudding

I love this hot chocolate. I buy it in New York City, and it comes in the most beautiful container. You can also get it online; see Sources. It's great to keep in your pantry for an impromptu dessert. I made 100 of these for my husband's birthday. It was like making chocolate soup, which I ladled into espresso cups, refrigerated, and adorned with whipped cream before serving. They are delicious, as well as being the easiest, richest dessert you'll ever make.

MAKES 1 ½ CUPS, SERVES 6 IN DEMITASSE CUPS

1½ cups MarieBelle hot chocolate powder
Whipped Cream (optional; page 145)

① In a large mixing bowl, mix the hot chocolate powder with 1 cup boiling water. Stir until smooth and evenly incorporated.

② Steam, simmer, or microwave for 20 to 40 seconds, until melted and smooth. (Be sure to use a microwave-safe bowl.)

③ Pour the mixture into ramekins or demitasse cups and chill in the refrigerator for 2 hours. Garnish with a dollop of whipped cream if desired.

The Nantucket Eight Ball

My favorite place in the whole world is Nantucket Island. I've worked there since I was a kid, from scooping ice cream and working at Que Sera Sarah to working as a private chef for families or as a short-order chef at the Sweet Shop (I was always standing on my tippy toes while making tuna melts or grilling a burger). Most nights at 10:00 P.M. I became a bouncer at the Boarding House, a restaurant and bar. The owners at the time, Bob Kuratek and Sarah Leah Chase, asked me to do the job because I knew most of the people on the island. I loved that job. Me, a little blonde-haired, freckled, five-foot-one, wise-ass girl, was asking everyone from ages seventeen to fifty for an ID—and that's where I go now for a Nantucket Eight Ball. At that time, the Boarding House was *the* place to be on the island.

SERVES 1

2 ounces Nantucket's own Triple Eight cranberry vodka or any cranberry vodka
1 ounce Rose's lime juice
1 lime wedge

Fill a glass with ice and pour in the vodka and lime juice. Garnish with the lime wedge.

MY FIRST DINNER PARTY: TACO NIGHT

Everyone loves a taco dinner, and it couldn't be easier for the host. (Some of the best parties I've thrown have been taco nights.) If you've never thrown a party or invited people over for dinner, this is the party for you: a great, casual dinner party to get the first-time host used to entertaining. The casual approach is ideal for your first time out; it will build your confidence when everyone has a great time.

If you have a round table, set it with a lazy Susan. Buy colorful paper napkins to give the table a little pizzazz. Orange, lime green, and navy blue are fun—I find the best colors and prices at IKEA. Most of these recipes can be prepared the day before; you can do things like chop the onions and tomatoes and shred the lettuce. Make the salad the night before (the orange salad dressing can also be used to flavor the taco meat). Get your bar ready: cut the limes and get the beer in the refrigerator. This will minimize any stress you're feeling about having people over.

The night of the party, just arrange the ingredients on a countertop, fry flour tortillas in oil, or buy blue-corn taco shells. Cook ground turkey or beef with a packet of seasoning, orange juice, and onions, and lay out the condiments in bowls. Have hot sauce ready too. (For any vegetarian guests, be sure to have extra condiments and black beans or refried beans so they can make vegetarian tacos.) Make sure the taco shells are warm and place them in a rectangular dish. About 5 minutes before you serve, heat the meat in a saucepan on high and stir it to keep it from burning. Transfer the hot meat to a bowl with a serving spoon. (If you haven't already, do yourself a favor and read "Parties R_x," page 5. It will really help you conquer your first dinner party!) Don't forget to offer them a Bambootini (page 237) or a Margarita (page 165) when they walk in the door to get them in the party mood.

And for dessert, who won't love an ice cream sundae bar? Save yourself a lot of trouble and buy everything: instead of making hot fudge, buy chocolate sauce, along with maraschino cherries, canned whipped cream (I like Land O'Lakes), Oreo cookies (you can even buy crushed Oreos), chopped walnuts or peanuts, and four flavors of ice cream (I like coffee, vanilla, caramel, and mint chocolate chip or plain chocolate). Serve the pints of ice cream in a bowl of ice or buy ice cream in 1-cup containers and let guests scoop their favorite flavor into a bowl (this is less messy than guests scooping from the large containers).

DINNER PARTY SHORTCUTS

I've been entertaining all my life, so I use lots of shortcuts for my parties, but they're even more essential if you're just learning to entertain. I find it easier to arrange the food in the kitchen and let guests go through a buffet line. This is especially true for a meal like this, where people like to customize their dinner. If you're really pressed for time, substitute shredded rotisserie chicken from the store for the turkey meat. (Follow the hostess guide on page 10 for more tricks and shortcuts.) And just remember, everyone is happy to be invited to someone else's house for dinner!

Lulu's Tip

For personal hostess gifts, order one of your favorite foods (a barbecue sauce or spice rub or coffee) and send it to your host as a thank you. Or bring a jar of homemade pesto.

Sweet and Spicy Tacos

These are always a big hit. I use three different kinds of meat in my taco mix, and the sausage really adds zing. And it's easy to throw together.

SERVES 10 TO 12

1 medium red onion, finely chopped

5 garlic cloves, minced

2 tablespoons extra virgin olive oil or unsalted butter

2 pounds ground turkey

1 pound ground beef

1 package sweet Italian sausage

2 bunches of scallions, both white and green parts, thinly sliced

1 bunch of fresh cilantro, finely chopped

3 tablespoons ground cumin

1 teaspoon chili powder

2 tablespoons Lawry's Seasoned Salt

¼ teaspoon ground pepper

1 tablespoon Tabasco sauce

¼ teaspoon cayenne

½ jalapeño pepper, minced

2½ cups orange juice

One 4.5-ounce package taco shells

One 12-ounce package 6-inch corn tortillas

4 tomatoes, chopped

2 heads romaine lettuce, chopped

2 onions, chopped

Chunky Guacamole (recipe follows) or avocado slices

One 12-ounce package shredded cheese

One 16-ounce carton sour cream

① In a large skillet over medium heat, sauté the onion and garlic in the olive oil or butter, stirring frequently, for 3 to 5 minutes, or until the onion is translucent.

② Add the ground turkey, beef, and sausage and cook, stirring, until the meat is browned.

③ Add the scallions, cilantro, cumin, chili powder, seasoned salt, pepper, Tabasco, cayenne, jalapeño, and orange juice and cook until the liquid has evaporated, about 4 minutes, stirring occasionally.

④ Remove the skillet from the heat and serve.

⑤ To prepare the tacos, lay out the taco shells, tortillas, and condiments (chopped tomatoes, lettuce, onions, guacamole, shredded cheese, and sour cream) and let guests assemble their own.

Chunky Guacamole

MAKES 2 CUPS; SERVES 6 TO 8

1 medium red onion, finely chopped

1 teaspoon honey

5 garlic cloves, minced

1 medium tomato, chopped (see Note)

½ cup finely chopped fresh cilantro

1 teaspoon salt

½ teaspoon ground pepper

1 teaspoon Tabasco sauce

5 large ripe avocados, pitted and peeled

Juice of ½ lemon or lime

Tortilla chips

① In a small bowl, combine the onion, honey, garlic, tomato, cilantro, salt, pepper, and Tabasco.

② Cover the bowl with a paper towel and leave it in the refrigerator for at least 1 hour to allow the flavors to meld.

③ In a medium bowl, mash the avocado with a fork and add it to the onion mixture. Add the lemon juice and stir to combine.

④ Serve with tortilla chips.

NOTE: Lay the chopped tomatoes on a paper towel to absorb any excess moisture or stir the excess liquid into the taco meat in the preceding recipe.

Lulu's Tip

Place the avocado pits in the guacamole to prevent it from turning brown. This guacamole is also delicious with chopped mango or apple.

Jícama-Citrus Salad
with Orange-Cilantro Dressing

Here's a crisp, fresh salad that's a wonderful complement to the spicy Taco Night food. This dressing can be used on any salad.

SERVES 4

FOR THE VINAIGRETTE

1 cup orange juice
½ cup roughly chopped fresh cilantro
1 garlic clove
1 tablespoon ground cumin
1½ teaspoons salt
⅛ teaspoon freshly ground black pepper
¼ cup extra virgin olive oil
¼ cup canola oil

FOR THE SALAD

1 large jícama, peeled and julienned
2 bunches of watercress, trimmed
2 oranges, peeled and segmented
1 small red onion, thinly sliced

① To make the vinaigrette, in a small saucepan over high heat, reduce the orange juice by half. Let cool.

② In a blender, combine the cilantro, garlic, cumin, salt, pepper, and reduced orange juice. With the blender still running, slowly pour the oils through the top and blend until the vinaigrette has emulsified.

③ In a large bowl, combine the jícama, watercress, oranges, and onion and toss to combine.

④ Add the vinaigrette and toss. Serve immediately.

Ice Cream Sundae Bar

This dessert bar is the perfect treat for every child, mom, dad, cousin, and grandparent—it puts a smile on people's faces. Be creative and think back to when you were a kid. What did you like to put on your ice cream?

SERVES 12

2 cups each of your favorite fudge, chocolate, and butterscotch sauce

2 cups fresh Whipped Cream (page 145) or 1 can prepared whipped cream

2 cups favorite nuts, coarsely chopped

2 pints fresh strawberries, sliced

6 bananas, sliced

2 cups crushed Heath Bars, Oreos, or gingersnap cookies

One 16-ounce jar maraschino cherries

Assorted sprinkles

3 half-gallon cartons ice cream, in assorted flavors (be sure to include vanilla)

① Warm the sauces on the stovetop or in the microwave and pour them into small pitchers.

② Place the toppings in assorted festive bowls.

③ Let the ice cream sit out for 15 minutes before serving so that it's easier to scoop.

Bambootini

My husband's cousins introduced me to the Bambootini, their favorite drink. They make pitchers of it and stick them in the fridge. This is perfect for Taco Night because it includes tequila and lime juice; think of it as a margarita with a twist!

SERVES 1

2 tablespoons tequila
2 tablespoons pomegranate juice
1 teaspoon Patrón Citrónge
2 tablespoons freshly squeezed lime juice

Shake all the ingredients with ice in a cocktail shaker and strain into a martini glass or in a tall glass over ice.

SUGAR HIGH SHINDIG

Having a dessert party makes your guests feel like kids in a candy store: for one night only they feel free to indulge in whatever sweets come their way. If you're a baker, this is the party for you. Make four or five great desserts, put out pots of coffee and a few coffee cocktails along with an assortment of liqueurs and whiskey, and get ready for the sugar rush. If you don't bake, there are so many great bakeries out there that you could throw this party for under $100, even if you buy all the goodies. Arranging a few platters of desserts and drinks makes this an easy party for the novice host or hostess.

While this is a great nighttime party, it also makes an indulgent afternoon affair. Dessert-based cocktails like Irish coffee, chocolate martinis, and hot chocolate with Frangelico replace the usual drinks but still let people indulge. You could also serve Bailey's on ice or a Bailey's milkshake that doubles as a dessert (or even a mood booster).

Nowadays there are so many people going gluten free that it's thoughtful to offer a gluten-free treat to your guests who adhere to gluten-free diets. Look for gluten-free breads, sweets, and scone mixes in specialty food and health food stores, but if you can't find them, store- or bakery-bought meringues are a quick and easy gluten-free treat. Many Web sites sell gluten-free treats, and Whole Foods carries a huge selection.

Easy Baking Shortcuts

Baking doesn't have to be done the day of the party. You can bake and freeze cookies and cakes weeks ahead of time. With cake, just let it defrost for a couple of hours on the countertop and then frost it the day of the party. Patty P's Chocolate Cake (page 220) freezes well unglazed; it will keep up to 1 month. Most supermarkets sell great ready-made puff pastry brands (in sheets and cups) and pie shells in the freezer sections, which makes baking and quick desserts a snap. (I prefer the Pepperidge Farm brand.) I like to serve small puff pastry cups filled with pudding, chocolate mousse, ice cream, or fresh fruit and whipped cream.

A Chocolate Primer

With so many varieties of chocolate in the baking aisle, it can be hard to choose. Of course, all chocolate comes from the cacao bean, which is then roasted and turned into a paste made of cocoa butter and cocoa solids. Where the beans come from, how they're roasted, and the types and amounts of additives used, however, determine the quality, flavor, and price of chocolate. Here are a few basics to help you pick the best chocolate for a recipe.

There are four types of dark chocolate: unsweetened, bittersweet, semisweet, and sweet:

* **Unsweetened:** Also called *baking* or *bitter chocolate*, this is the purest chocolate you can get, with nothing added. By U.S. law, it must contain between 50 and 58 percent cocoa butter. It's used only for baking, as the flavor is too bitter to eat straight.

* **Bittersweet:** Chocolate makers add sugar, lecithin, and vanilla to create bittersweet chocolate. The more cocoa solids used and the less sugar, the more bitter the flavor.

* **Semisweet:** This variety contains sugar, lecithin, and vanilla and a bit more sugar than bittersweet—and also less fat.

* **Sweet:** This contains sugar, lecithin, and vanilla and a bit more sugar than semisweet chocolate.

There are two other common chocolate varieties that fall on the sweeter side:

* **Milk:** Chocolate makers add dry milk to sweetened chocolate to create milk chocolate, most often used in chocolate bars.

* **White:** This isn't actually chocolate. Sugar, cocoa butter, milk solids, lecithin (for texture), and vanilla are common ingredients that make up white "chocolate."

Store your chocolate in a cool (60°F to 70°F), dry place, tightly wrapped. Stored properly, dark chocolate can last up to ten years. (Milk and white chocolates have a shorter shelf life due to the milk solids; they'll keep for only about nine months.) Chocolate doesn't technically go bad, but if it's stored improperly, the flavor and/or texture can be affected.

Quick chocolate substitutions

* 3 tablespoons unsweetened cocoa plus 1 tablespoon butter equals 1 ounce unsweetened chocolate.

* ½ ounce unsweetened chocolate plus 1 tablespoon granulated sugar equals 1 ounce semisweet chocolate.

* ½ cup plus 1 tablespoon unsweetened cocoa, ¼ cup plus 3 tablespoons granulated sugar, and 3 tablespoons butter combine to equal 6 ounces semisweet chocolate chips.

Feel free to use bittersweet and semisweet chocolate interchangeably in recipes, but never substitute milk and white chocolate—they contain milk protein, which will change the flavor and texture of the recipe. When melting chocolate, be sure to melt it on low heat (preferably in a double boiler) because it scorches easily.

Double-Chocolate Cookies

These intensely chocolaty cookies are my only brother Byrne's favorites.

MAKES 24 COOKIES

6 ounces unsweetened chocolate

1⅓ cups sugar

8 tablespoons (1 stick) unsalted butter, cut into pieces

2 large eggs

1 tablespoon instant espresso powder or 1 tablespoon strong brewed coffee

1 tablespoon vanilla extract

1 cup all-purpose flour

2 tablespoons Droste Dutch cocoa powder

2 cups semisweet chocolate chips

½ teaspoon salt

① Preheat the oven to 350°F. Grease 2 baking sheets or line them with Silpat baking mats.

② Place the unsweetened chocolate and the sugar into the bowl of a food processor and process for 3 minutes. The mixture should be superfine.

③ Add the butter, eggs, espresso, and vanilla and blend, scraping down the bowl once. Pulse twice.

④ Add the flour, cocoa, chocolate chips, and salt. Pulse just until combined.

⑤ Using a ⅓-cup measuring cup, scoop the dough into mounds about 2 inches apart on the baking sheets.

⑥ Bake for 10 to 12 minutes. Let cool for 2 minutes and then carefully transfer to a serving tray. They can be frozen for up to 1 month; defrost at room temperature before serving.

Lulu's Coconut Cupcakes

My love for coconut started when I had my first Mounds bar. These satisfy anybody's sweet tooth.

MAKES 24 CUPCAKES

FOR THE CAKE

One 18-ounce package white cake mix

3 large eggs

8 tablespoons (1 stick) salted butter, melted

1 teaspoon vanilla extract

1 teaspoon salt

1 teaspoon coconut extract or coconut syrup

One 3-ounce package instant vanilla pudding mix or 1 cup sour cream can be substituted

2 cups sweetened dried flaked coconut

FOR THE FROSTING

¾ pound (3 sticks) salted butter, at room temperature

One 8-ounce package cream cheese, at room temperature

4 cups confectioners' sugar

2 teaspoons freshly squeezed lemon juice

1 teaspoon salt

1 teaspoon vanilla extract

1 tablespoon plus 1 teaspoon coconut extract or coconut syrup

① Preheat the oven to 350°F.

② Put the cake mix, eggs, melted butter, vanilla, salt, coconut extract, instant pudding mix, coconut, and 1¼ cups water into a large bowl. Beat with a hand mixer on medium speed for 2 minutes, occasionally scraping down the sides of the bowl.

③ Pour the batter into two greased 12-cup muffin tins or tins lined with muffin cups. Bake for 18 to 20 minutes, or until a toothpick inserted into the middle of a cupcake comes out clean. Let the cupcakes cool completely before frosting.

④ To make the frosting, beat the butter and cream cheese together until well blended. Add the sugar, lemon juice, salt, vanilla, and coconut extract and mix well.

NOTE: You can make the cupcakes 1 day ahead; just keep them in an airtight container. They also freeze well, unfrosted.

Patty Powers's Strawberry Tart

This tart is so delicious that Joan from Joan's on Third, a beloved Los Angeles gourmet marketplace and café, wanted the recipe. Light and luscious, it's perfect with summer strawberries.

**MAKES ONE 8-INCH TART (SERVING 6 TO 8)
OR ONE 12-INCH TART (SERVING 12 TO 14)**

FOR ONE 8-INCH CRUST
1 cup all-purpose flour
8 tablespoons (1 stick) unsalted butter
3 tablespoons confectioners' sugar

FOR ONE 12-INCH CRUST
1½ cups all-purpose flour
12 tablespoons (1½ sticks) unsalted butter
4½ tablespoons confectioners' sugar

FILLING FOR ONE 8-INCH TART
3 ounces cream cheese, softened
1 tablespoon freshly squeezed lemon juice
1 teaspoon lemon zest
½ cup granulated sugar
1 cup heavy cream
2 pints strawberries, hulled

FILLING FOR ONE 12-INCH TART
4½ ounces cream cheese, softened
1½ tablespoons freshly squeezed lemon juice
1½ teaspoons grated lemon zest
¾ cup granulated sugar
1½ cups heavy cream
2 pints strawberries, hulled

FOR THE GLAZE
½ cup (4 ounces) currant jelly
2 tablespoons kirsch or Triple Sec

① Preheat the oven to 350°F.

② To make the crust, in the bowl of a food processor, combine the flour, butter, and sugar. Pulse eight times to combine and then run the food processor for about 30 seconds, until a ball of dough forms.

③ Wrap the dough in plastic wrap and refrigerate for 20 minutes.

④ Remove the chilled dough from the refrigerator and press it into the sides and bottom of an 8- or 12-inch springform pan. Prick the bottom of the crust with a fork. Bake the crust for 15 minutes, or until golden brown, and let cool completely.

⑤ To make the filling, combine the cream cheese, lemon juice, zest, sugar, and cream using a hand or standing mixer.

6. Pour the filling into the crust. Refrigerate the tart until set, about 45 minutes.

7. Arrange the strawberries in a pretty pattern on top of the tart.

8. Melt the currant jelly in a saucepan over low heat and add the kirsch or Triple Sec.

9. Brush the glaze over the strawberries with a pastry brush.

NOTE: You can make the tart the day before you plan to serve it. Wrap it in plastic wrap and refrigerate.

Lemon Dreams

My mother's dear friend Anita Flynn makes these delicious little cookie dreams. If you put them on your tongue, they'll melt—they're that light. She kindly gave me the recipe.

MAKES 48 COOKIES

FOR THE COOKIES

½ pound (2 sticks) salted butter, at room temperature

¼ cup plus 2 tablespoons confectioners' sugar

¾ cup cornstarch

1 cup all-purpose flour

FOR THE FROSTING

3 tablespoons salted butter, at room temperature

1 cup confectioners' sugar

1 tablespoon orange juice

1 teaspoon freshly squeezed lemon juice

① Preheat the oven to 375°F. Lightly grease a baking sheet or line it with a Silpat baking mat.

② To make the cookies, cream the butter and confectioners' sugar with an electric mixer until fluffy.

③ Stir in the cornstarch and flour and mix well.

④ For each cookie, use about 1 tablespoon of dough. Using your palms, roll the dough into small balls and place them on the baking sheet 1 inch apart.

⑤ Bake the cookies for 7 to 11 minutes, or until lightly golden. Let the cookies cool completely on the baking sheet.

⑥ To make the frosting, in a medium bowl, cream the butter and sugar with an electric mixer. Slowly mix in the orange and lemon juices and mix until smooth.

⑦ Let the cookies cool completely on the baking sheet. Place the frosting in a pastry bag fitted with a star tip and frost the tops. The cookies will keep for a week in a sealed container.

Irish Coffee

You don't have to be Irish to like this.

SERVES 1

2 ounces Bushmills Irish whiskey
2 teaspoons packed brown sugar
5 to 6 ounces freshly brewed strong black coffee
2 tablespoons Whipped Cream (page 145)
Shaved chocolate and a cinnamon stick

① In a tall, heatproof glass, combine the whiskey and sugar and stir until the sugar is dissolved.

② Add the coffee.

③ Spoon the whipped cream on top and garnish with the chocolate and cinnamon stick.

Coffee Milk Shakes

I love coffee anything. These shakes are great served with malt balls on the side—simply fill paper cupcake liners with them.

SERVES 8 IN TALL GLASSES, 16 IN SHOT GLASSES

8 scoops coffee ice cream
1½ cups whole milk
1½ cups ice cubes
¼ cup plus 2 tablespoons
   malted-milk powder

Combine all the ingredients in a blender on high until smooth. Pour into 8 tall glasses or 16 shot glasses. Serve immediately.

RETRO GAME NIGHT

Everyone relishes the chance to feel like a kid again, and what better way than to host a Saturday game night, with retro games like Twister and Operation and a retro food spread? I threw a 1950s party for one celebrity client, and it was quite a night: we served chicken liver pâté with vegetables, deviled eggs, and taco tartlets (made with ground beef, Cheddar cheese, sour cream, and tortilla chips). I even served White Castle hamburgers that I bought at my local supermarket.

This game night menu is inspired by what is now considered retro: Swedish meatballs with creamy dill sauce alongside old-fashioned Velveeta dip. Old standbys like meat loaf, chicken pot pies, and butterscotch pudding are unexpected pleasures that people love, and a colorful assortment of sherbets makes the perfect retro finish to the meal. Serve the food on a buffet table and let people graze or, for a fun twist, arrange the food on old-fashioned plastic TV trays in lime green.

Have guests come dressed in 1970s outfits (and have a prize ready for the best costume). Or visit a vintage store and purchase some groovy hats, shoes, and other accessories for people to try on. Although I'm not a big fan of party favors, give a great box of chocolates, a great drink or cocktail book, or a Slinky to the person with the best costume.

And don't forget to put on music to match the time period: get some 1970s or 1980s tunes to groove to while you break out the board games and play a round of Simon Says, Twister, or Life.

DÉCOR

Use bright colors to evoke a youthful 1970s or 1980s atmosphere: shades of green, orange, or yellow will set the scene. For table centerpieces, use a Magic 8-Ball (a favorite game from my childhood). Decorate the table with jacks or canisters of Pick-Up Stix. Use the Twister game mat as a tablecloth or on the bar to set the mood. Pull out other retro games to anchor the decoration for this party: Rubik's Cubes, tiddlywinks, Etch a Sketches, Slinkies, and yo-yos are fun to leave on the dinner or coffee table for people to play with.

Retro Bar

At parties like these, I love to serve colorful cocktails. The Screwdriver was big in the 1970s, as well as tropical drinks like the Fuzzy Navel, Mai Tai, and the Tequila Sunrise. Be sure to garnish the cocktails with swizzle sticks. Another very seventies drink is the Harvey Wallbanger, made with vodka, orange juice, and Galliano, an Italian anise liqueur. For a modern twist, make a fresh apple martini with freshly squeezed apple juice, vodka, and a splash of fresh lemon juice.

FROZEN LIME PUNCH

Another easy drink that looks great in a pitcher is Frozen Lime Punch. Fill the blender halfway with ice and add one 12-ounce can limeade, 1 can vodka, and 1 cup fresh mint leaves and blend until slushy. Add 1 can club soda or ginger ale if you need to stretch it. You can make it in batches and keep it in the refrigerator until ready to serve.

Lulu's Simply Divine Cheese Dip

This is my version of the classic Velveeta cheese dip—and it's the perfect excuse to break out your fondue pot. Serve this dip with corn chips, Fritos, or Cheez Doodles.

MAKES 2 CUPS

1 tablespoon unsalted butter

1 cup finely chopped onion

2 teaspoons sugar

2 garlic cloves, minced

1 teaspoon Lawry's Seasoned Salt

1 teaspoon salt

2 cups grated 4-cheese blend (preferably Mexican blend)

One 10-ounce can diced tomatoes with green chiles (I like RoTel brand)

¾ cup sour cream

2 teaspoons chili powder

1 teaspoon ground cumin

5 scallions, both white and green parts, thinly sliced

① Melt the butter in a large sauté pan over medium heat. Add the onion, sugar, garlic, seasoned salt, and salt and cook until the onion is translucent, about 5 minutes.

② Turn the heat to low and add the cheese, tomatoes, sour cream, chili powder, cumin, and scallions. Stir until melted. Serve warm.

Chicken Liver Pâté

Even if you don't like chicken liver pâté, try this one. Serve it as a spread with French bread, apple slices, or crackers.

MAKES 4 CUPS

1 cup almonds

8 medium shallots, sliced

4 garlic cloves, sliced

1 large onion, chopped

10 tablespoons unsalted butter

1 teaspoon sugar

3 large Granny Smith apples, peeled, cored, and quartered

1 pound chicken livers, trimmed and membranes removed

1 pound sweet Italian pork sausage

½ cup Calvados

One 8-ounce package cream cheese, at room temperature

2 teaspoons Lawry's Seasoned Salt

1 teaspoon white pepper

1 tablespoon chopped fresh tarragon

1 teaspoon ground allspice

1 tablespoon fresh thyme

2 teaspoons Tabasco Sauce

1 teaspoon hot red pepper flakes

① In the bowl of a food processor, pulse the almonds until coarsely chopped; remove and reserve.

② Add the shallots, garlic, and onion and process until finely chopped.

③ Melt 8 tablespoons (1 stick) of butter in a 10-inch skillet over medium-high heat. Add the sugar and the onion mixture.

④ Add the apples to the bowl of the food processor and pulse until finely chopped.

⑤ Add the chopped apples to the skillet and cook gently until the ingredients are soft and translucent, about 10 minutes. Transfer the mixture to a large bowl.

⑥ Melt the remaining 2 tablespoons of butter in the skillet. Add the chicken livers and sausage, breaking up the sausage with a fork, and sauté over medium-high heat until nearly cooked through, about 10 minutes.

⑦ Turn the heat to high, add the Calvados, and cook for 2 minutes.

⑧ Transfer the meat mixture to the food processor, add the apple and onion mixture, and process for 30 seconds, stopping once to scrape down the sides of the bowl.

⑨ Add the cream cheese, seasoned salt, pepper, tarragon, allspice, thyme, Tabasco, and red pepper flakes and process until smooth, stopping once to scrape down the sides of the bowl. Add the almonds and pulse 5 or 6 times.

⑩ Let the pâté cool. Cover with plastic wrap and refrigerate for at least
   4 hours and up to 7 days.

NOTE: You can freeze the pâté for up to 1 month. You can make the pâté in any
shape you like. I made two heart-shaped pâtés for one party and I served it in
mini ramekins.

Sweet Pea Puree

My sister Sue makes this at least once a week. It is even good served
cold, as a dip.

MAKES 1 ½ CUPS; SERVES 4

One 16-ounce package frozen peas
½ cup chicken stock
1 tablespoon unsalted butter
1 teaspoon salt
½ teaspoon freshly ground black pepper
¼ cup julienned fresh mint

① Combine the peas and stock in a small saucepan. Bring to a boil and
   simmer for 1 minute. Do not overcook.

② Remove from the heat and transfer the peas and stock to a food
   processor.

③ Add the butter, salt, pepper, and mint and puree until smooth.

Turkey Meat Loaf with Chili Aïoli

Rich, moist, and tangy, this meat loaf is even better the next day. The spicy aïoli sets it apart from ordinary meat loaf.

FOR THE MEAT LOAF

1 to 1¼ pounds ground turkey or ground beef

½ pound sweet or spicy Italian sausage, casings removed

½ cup Chili Aïoli (recipe follows)

½ cup ketchup

¼ cup barbecue sauce

5 garlic cloves, crushed

¼ cup minced red onion

¼ cup chopped fresh cilantro

½ cup peeled and grated Idaho potato (from about 1 small potato)

1 tablespoon lime juice

2 teaspoons salt

1 teaspoon freshly ground black pepper

1 cup shredded fontina cheese

FOR THE TOPPING

¼ cup barbecue sauce

¼ cup ketchup

① To make the meat loaf, in a large bowl, combine the turkey, sausage, ½ cup of the aïoli, the ketchup, barbecue sauce, garlic, onion, cilantro, potato, lime juice, salt, and pepper and mix until well incorporated.

② Remove half the mixture and form it into a loaf on a jelly-roll pan.

③ Pat the cheese evenly on top and then press the remaining meat loaf mixture on top.

④ For the topping, mix the ketchup and the barbecue sauce together and brush generously over the meat loaf.

⑤ Bake for 50 minutes, or until nicely browned. Serve with a dollop of Chili Aïoli.

Chili Aïoli

MAKES 1 ½ CUPS

½ cup sour cream
½ cup mayonnaise
2 teaspoons chili powder
1 teaspoon barbecue sauce
3 garlic cloves, minced
1 teaspoon sriracha sauce, 1 teaspoon
   Tabasco sauce, or ½ teaspoon chili oil

2 tablespoons freshly squeezed lemon
   juice
1 teaspoon sugar
2 teaspoons Lawry's Seasoned Salt
3 scallions, both white and green parts,
   thinly sliced
¼ cup finely chopped fresh cilantro

Mix all the ingredients in a mixing bowl until smooth. Store in the refrigerator for up to 1 week.

Cauliflower Puree

MAKES 3 CUPS; SERVES 6 TO 8

3 cups chicken stock
1 head of cauliflower, cut into pieces
4 tablespoons (½ stick) salted butter
2 teaspoons white truffle oil

1 teaspoon freshly grated nutmeg
   or ½ teaspoon ground nutmeg
¼ cup grated Parmesan cheese
Salt and pepper to taste

1. Bring the chicken stock to a boil in a medium saucepan over medium heat and add the cauliflower. Cook the cauliflower until tender, about 10 minutes.

2. Drain in a colander and place in the bowl of a food processor along with the butter, truffle oil, nutmeg, and Parmesan. Process until smooth and season with salt and pepper to taste. Serve hot.

Butterscotch Pudding with Rum Sauce

In Los Angeles, I ate at the most delicious pizzeria restaurant called Mozza, owned by Nancy Silverton and Mario Batali. I tried their butterscotch pudding—it was so good I went to the moon and back! I savored every bite. This recipe is my version. I think it's close, and I hope you have the same reaction I did at Pizzeria Mozza.

SERVES 10

5 tablespoons salted butter

1 cup packed brown sugar

1½ teaspoons kosher salt

2 cups heavy cream

1 cup milk

1 tablespoon Scotch

1 tablespoon rum

1 teaspoon vanilla extract

1 large egg

2 large egg yolks

3 tablespoons cornstarch

Rum Sauce (recipe follows)

Maldon sea salt or other flaky sea salt

Whipped Cream (page 145)

10 cinnamon sticks (optional)

① In a large saucepan, melt the butter over very low heat.

② Add the sugar and salt and stir over medium heat until the mixture is smooth and begins to bubble. Cook for 3 to 5 minutes, or until thick.

③ Slowly stir in the cream. When the cream has been fully incorporated, stir in the milk, Scotch, rum, and vanilla. Remove from the heat and set aside.

④ In a small bowl, whisk the egg, egg yolks, and cornstarch together until smooth.

⑤ Whisk 1 cup of the cream mixture slowly into the eggs to temper them. (This will prevent the eggs from curdling.) Add the tempered mixture back to the saucepan and whisk to combine.

⑥ Place the saucepan over medium-high heat and whisk constantly for 3 to 5 minutes. When the mixture begins to bubble, turn the heat to low and continue stirring as it thickens.

⑦ Remove the pan from the heat and pour the mixture through a fine-mesh strainer into a mixing bowl.

⑧ Cover with plastic wrap to prevent a skin from forming on top and let cool to room temperature. Place the pudding in the refrigerator.

⑨ Divide the pudding among 10 small glasses and serve with 1 tablespoon rum sauce, a sprinkle of sea salt, a dollop of whipped cream, and a cinnamon stick.

Rum Sauce

MAKES 1 ½ CUPS

1 cup packed dark brown sugar
½ cup dark corn syrup
½ cup heavy cream
4 tablespoons (½ stick) unsalted butter
¼ cup golden rum
1 teaspoon vanilla extract

1. Combine the brown sugar, corn syrup, cream, and butter in a heavy medium saucepan.

2. Bring to a low boil over medium-high heat and cook for 10 minutes.

3. Remove from the heat and stir in the rum and vanilla.

4. Let cool to room temperature.

NOTE: You can make the sauce up to a month in advance, storing it in a glass jar in the refrigerator. Reheat in a microwave or over a double boiler before serving.

Ivy Gimlet

Be careful: you can get hooked on these! They're inspired by the famous celebrity watering hole in L.A., The Ivy.

SERVES 1

1 lime, cut into wedges
2 teaspoons sugar
10 fresh mint leaves
2 to 2½ ounces vodka

① Place 2 lime wedges in an old-fashioned or small highball glass.

② Add the sugar and mint to the glasses and muddle them.

③ Pour in the desired amount of vodka and stir.

④ Add crushed ice (regular ice cubes are fine too), stir, and serve.

LULU'S ENTERTAINING CHEAT SHEET

THE DOUBLE-CHECK CHECKLIST

Run through these questions to help you plan a party or as a last-minute checklist. You can make a copy of this page, laminate it, and then use a wax pencil to check off items. Just wipe it off when you're done, and it's ready for your next event! Tape it next to your emergency numbers inside your kitchen cabinet.

FOOD
○ Are all the dishes prepared?
○ Is your oven preheated, if necessary?
○ Are the cheeses out at room temperature?
○ Did you put out the cocktail snacks, like potato chips or nuts?
○ Is the table set? Are your place cards written?
○ Do you have enough plates and silverware for all the courses, including dessert and coffee?
○ Are water glasses on the table?
○ Is there a bottle or pitcher of water on the table and one in the fridge, ready to go?
○ Do you have a take-out menu ready in case of emergency?
○ Is your dessert ready? Do you have bowls of candy on hand, such as malt balls, M&M's, and chocolate bars broken into small pieces?

MUSIC
○ Are your iPod playlists ready? Is your iPod charged?
○ Do you have your party CDs out, or do you have a satellite radio on?

MISCELLANEOUS
○ Do you have a wine and beer opener handy?
○ Do you have garbage bags and extra paper towels?
○ Is the number of a taxi company or car service nearby?
○ Do you have a broom and dustpan ready?
○ Is there extra toilet paper in the bathroom?
○ Do you have disinfectant wipes under the bathroom sink?

DECORATION
○ Do you have candles and matches or a lighter wand?
○ Are your lights dimmed?
○ Did you finish staging your house with visual accents such as a bowl of apples, an orchid plant, or a vase of flowers? Do a quick walk-through of every room.
○ Do you have a scented candle ready in the bathroom?

DRINKS
○ Do you have enough glasses?
○ Do you have ice?
○ Are there extra paper cups in the pantry?
○ Have you stocked the bar with lemons and limes?
○ Do you have the proper drinks and mixers on hand?
○ Do you have the needed garnishes, such as olives?
○ Do you have cocktail napkins?
○ Are the white wine, beer, and bottled water chilled?

THE TWENTY-TWO-MINUTE COUNTDOWN
○ Candles lit?
○ Music on?
○ Bar set up?
○ Wine uncorked?
○ Are you dressed?
○ Outdoor lights on and entry path clean and inviting?
○ Bathrooms clean and stocked?

SOURCES

HOUSEWARES

ANTHROPOLOGIE
A national chain of stores with great housewares and accessories.
anthropologie.com

BODUM
Makers of coffee accessories and my favorite coffee press.
bodum.com

CRATE & BARREL
Wonderful source of inexpensive housewares.
crateandbarrel.com

EARTH FRIENDLY PRODUCTS
An environmentally friendly company that makes my favorite parsley spray and other household products. Available online and at major retailers.
ecos.com

FRUITS-PASSION
Maker of Cucina brand, a great-smelling line of hand lotions, room sprays, aroma sticks, and soaps. Available online and at major retailers.
fruits-passion.com
800-276-9952

HOME GOODS
A national chain of houseware stores, selling everything from cutting boards and serving pieces to rugs and lamps.
homegoods.com

IKEA
One of my favorite places for party supplies like paper napkins and serving trays.
ikea.com

MRS. MEYER'S CLEANING PRODUCTS
Great-smelling, all-natural household cleaners and sprays, available at many supermarkets.
mrsmeyers.com

NORMANN COPENHAGEN
A Danish housewares company with innovative kitchen supplies and housewares.
normann-copenhagen.com

PROGRESSIVE INTERNATIONAL
A specialty cookware maker whose products are available through various kitchen and home stores.
progressiveintl.com

WILLIAMS-SONOMA
They sell my favorite inexpensive milk frother, along with hundreds of other amazing items.
williams-sonoma.com

WISTERIA
A great online and catalog source for decorative items.
www.wisteria.com
800-320-9757

ENTERTAINING SUPPLIES

BAMBU
I love bamboo plates, platters, and accessories from Bambu. They also produce a line of Veneerware, a great alternative to paper plates. Available online and at retailers like Whole Foods, Crate & Barrel, and Sur La Table.
bambuhome.com

BLOOMINGDALES
Bloomingdales has all your entertaining necessities.
bloomingdales.com

BROOKE BOOTHE DESIGN
Nantucket Monogram
LInens, Gifts and Stationery
www.brookeboothedesign.com
508-228-6006

CASPARI
A great entertaining supply company with beautiful paper products, including paper plates, napkins, and gift wrap. Their products are sold at retailers and upscale supermarkets.
casparionline.com
800-CASPARI (227-7274)

DAPHNE F. MITCHELL STATIONERY
Personalized stationery and gifts, based in Connecticut.
203-913-2758

HAPPY KIDS
Online source for personalized gift items and children's party favors.
happykidspersonalized.com
800-543-7687

LILLIAN VERNON
Great retailer and catalog for gifts.
lillianvernon.com
800-901-9402

MAIL ORDER MOMMY
Online retailer for great party supplies and personalized items.
mailordermommy.com

ORIENTAL TRADING COMPANY
An online party supply store with party supplies, craft, and novelty items.
orientaltrading.com

PACIFIC MERCHANTS TRADING COMPANY
This online retailer specializes in wooden serving pieces and tableware.
pacificmerchants.com
818-988-8999

PEARL RIVER MART
A Chinese-American department store in New York City with a wide selection of Asian tableware, clothing, accessories, and food.
477 Broadway, New York, NY
pearlriver.com

PUTUMAYO WORLD MUSIC
This great source for world music with CD compilations for adults and kids is available at many music stores and bookstores and online.
putumayo.com
888-PUTUMAYO

SENSATIONS TABLEWARE
This company sells bamboo skewers, table linens, paper plates, and small plastic spoons in a variety of colors.
sensationstableware.com

SWEET PEA DESIGNS
A source for stylish invitations.
sweetpeadesigns.com

TABLETOPICS
This company makes preprinted cards on various topics available as coasters, cards, or place cards that are great conversation starters. You can also order custom topics.
tabletopics.com
888-690-6001

TABLE TOSS
This New York City company sells pretty, sassy reusable tabletop accessories such as coasters, place mats, place cards, and napkin holders.
tabletoss.com
212-769-2577

TARGET
Target has everything you need and more at affordable prices.
target.com

VALSEY AND ME
Their custom soaps make great party or wedding favors.
http://valseyandme.com

FOOD PRODUCTS

AMAZON.COM
A source for demitasse sugar sticks, also called *rock-sugar sticks,* which are a fun way to liven up coffee or tea. Also available at many gourmet shops.

BÉQUET CONFECTIONS
An artisanal producer of candy, cookies, and chocolates based in Montana. I love to sprinkle salts from Saltistry on top of their caramels.
bequetconfections.com
877-423-7838

BROADWAY PANHANDLER
Fabulous cookware store in New York City.
65 East 8th Street, New York, NY
broadwaypanhandler.com
866-266-5927

CHEESE STORE OF BEVERLY HILLS
My favorite cheese shop—they carry cheeses from all over the world.
cheesestorebh.com
310-278-2855

CUSTOM FORTUNE COOKIES
This company makes personalized fortune cookies.
customfortunecookies.com
713-988-2542

FISH TALES SEAFOOD COMPANY
My favorite seafood shop in New Canaan, Connecticut. Ask for Houston!
203-966-6300

FRAN'S CHOCOLATES
This small candy company, based in Seattle, makes wonderful chocolates.
franschocolate.com
800-422-3726

GROOVY CANDIES
An online store featuring hundreds of hard-to-find candies.
groovycandies.com
888-729-1960

H&H BAGELS
A New York City institution that ships bagels around the world.
hhbagels.com
800-692-2435

THE HONEY BAKED HAM COMPANY
honeybakedham.com
866-492-HAMS

LEGAL SEAFOODS
A Boston-based seafood company with restaurants and mail-order seafood, including clambakes.
legalseafoods.com
800-343-5804

LOBEL'S
A great source for spiral-cut hams, as well as other meats.
lobels.com
877-783-4512

MURRAY'S CHEESE SHOP
This fabulous cheese shop in Manhattan carries a wide variety of cheeses.
murrayscheese.com
888-692-4339, extension 7

NEWSOM'S AGED KENTUCKY COUNTRY HAMS
newsomscountryham.com
270-365-2482

PETROSSIAN
One of the best fine food sources in the United States, Petrossian is my favorite place to buy caviar.
petrossian.com
800-828-9241

JOHN KELLY CHOCOLATES
1506 N. Sierra Bonita Ave., Los Angeles
johnkellychocolates.com
800-609-4243

QUALITY FRESH SEAFOOD
A Massachusetts-based seafood company that sells fresh seafood and clambakes.
qualityfreshseafood.com
888-205-8848

RAYE'S FROM MAINE
Handcrafted specialty mustards.
rayesmustard.com
800-853-1903

SALTISTRY
Handcrafted specialty salts made
by Chef Joni Fay Hill.
saltistry.com

SILVERBOW
A honey company that sells a variety of
flavored honey sticks, another great way
to flavor coffee or tea.
silverbowhoney.com
866-44-HONEY

THREE DOG BAKERY
A national chain of dog bakeries.
threedog.com

TUPPERWARE
Great source of kitchen items, with everything from storage containers and cook's
tools to serving items and Popsicle molds.
http://order.tupperware.com/coe/app/home
800-366-3800

WILLIAMS-SONOMA
Wonderful mail-order croissants and
breakfast pastries arrive frozen and can
be baked as needed.
williams-sonoma.com

YOGHUND
Maker of organic frozen-yogurt treats
for dogs.
yoghund.com
877-964-4863

BEVERAGES

JONES SODA
This small beverage company makes fun
sodas in flavors like Orange Creamsicle and
Blue Bubblegum. You can also custom-
order Jones Soda with your own photo on
the label, which is fun to do for a birthday
or anniversary party. Available at most
supermarkets and online.
jonessoda.com
800-656-6050

LE PALAIS DES THÉS
A French tea company with tea salons
in France and Beverly Hills.
palaisdesthes.com/en/

**MARIEBELLE
HOT CHOCOLATE**
A specialty chocolate company based
in New York City.
484 Broome Street
New York, NY
212-925-6999
mariebelle.com

MIGHTY LEAF
A specialty tea company whose teas are
available at grocery stores nationwide and
through its Web site.
mightyleaf.com

MOJITO ISLAND
This small southern California drink company makes a great, all-natural drink mixer
that can be used for mixed drinks or nonalcoholic mocktails.
mojitoisland.com

SONOMA SYRUP COMPANY
A specialty syrup company with a wide
range of flavors; available at specialty
retailers and through the Web site.
SonomaSyrup.com

THINK COFFEE
A small coffee company based in New York City that sells environmentally friendly coffee and fine teas.
248 Mercer Street
New York, NY
thinkcoffeenyc.com
212-228-6226

TORANI SYRUPS
Flavored syrups, available at many food retailers and supermarkets.
torani.com

URTH CAFFE
An organic café in Los Angeles that sells delicious coffee and teas.
urthcaffe.com

RENTALS

CARL'S JR.
A hamburger chain that rents mobile catering trucks.
877-799-7827
carlsjr.com

IN-N-OUT
A California hamburger chain that rents mobile burger trucks called *cookout trailers.*
626-813-8295
in-n-out.com

MISCELLANEOUS

THURSDAY PLANTATION
Sells tea-tree toothpicks, a great alternative to gum; available online and at some health-food stores.
thursdayplantation.com

WINEAWAY
A solution that gets rid of red wine stains. Available at some wine stores, home, and cooking stores.
evergreenlabs.com
888-946-3292

ACKNOWLEDGMENTS

First and foremost I want to thank my family on the East Coast and my friends who have become my family on the West Coast. My husband, Stephen Danelian, whose unique zest for life and creativity is beyond. "Enjoy the process," as he would say. I could have never done this beautiful book without you. Your encouragement, coffee, and taste testing went beyond the call of duty. I love you, buddy!

To my sisters and brother, who were only a phone call away listening to me laugh and cry throughout this whole book process.

To Laura Holmes Haddad, for helping me shape this book and understanding "the Lulu language"—what I really meant to say. Congrats—you caught on fast. Thank you for sitting through the endless hours of Grand Central Station at Lindenhurst and bringing this book to fruition. What a great fete the two of us had; it was great working with you.

To my dear friend Leslie Rubinoff—you are a gem for your continued support throughout this process, and your daily phone calls were a gift.

Martha Riley—it all started at 61 Hulbert Avenue.

Leslie Berge—thanks for all your input.

To Johnathan Wilber—you're the honchos, ponchos . . . thanks, buddy!

To Nicky Woo—you're the epitome of cool. Thank you for always saying "okay."

All the Danelians, Landeses, Steins, and Segels—kisses to you all!

To Littia Serrano—thanks for always just being there and running with it. You're the best. I love you!

The Bell clan—great kids! Fun family! Old friends! Thank you!

The Killians—What would I do without you? I love you very much!

Thanks to the Island of Nantucket, where I really realized I was a chef.

To my father, who would have been so proud and who would have gotten "lots of mileage" that his Lulu had written a book. Wish you were here to see it.

To my mother, who made me look at everything from a beautiful point of view, and whose passion for cooking I inherited.

To EGV, who told me I needed to do a book.

To my new friend Lisa Masuda, the voice of reason. I had never met someone who was so calm, cool, collected, and an utter delight to be around. Thank you for deciphering my fly-by-the-seat-of-my-pants cooking style and turning the dishes into recipes. I could have never done it without you.

To Brettne Bloom, my agent, for believing in me.

To my new friend David Sweeney— you are a class act.

To my editor, Cassie Jones, who let me be me. You've become my friend. Thank you for that.

To Stephen Danelian— your pictures are sublime; there are no words to express my thanks! Just know "you're the boss, applesauce." I love you, buddy!

Special thanks to my friends who graciously opened their homes.

Molly Powers and the whole Kellogg family—who else would get up at 4:00 a.m. to dig steamers? Thank you for helping us make our first photo shoot a reality. You went above and beyond the call of duty.

The Parisian Perrins—there is no one else who is as "cool" as their house.

Ronak—Wahoo to you!

To Miro, the dependable Bulgarian. Thanks, buddy, for always cooking with a smile on your face. And without your muscles Lisa and I would have broken our backs running back and forth from the kitchen throughout all our catering jobs and photo shoots. You are a good egg, my friend. Thank you, Miro Darling! (a term of endearment "team Lulu" picked up from Arianna Huffington).

CZ—thanks for all your encouragment. XFGM.

To my copyeditor, Chris Benton—thanks! You made me think, hey, it's gonna be all right. People may actually buy this book.

To my inspirations: my mother, Sarah Leah Chase, Julia Child, Patti Altman, Martha Stewart, Ina Garten (the Barefoot Contessa), Nancy Silverton, Ruth Reichl, and Mark Bittman.

Mary McDonald and John Berchi—I love you two like my sister and brother. Thank you for always being there.

Sally Horchow and Paco— your entertaining prowess is contagious.

Ela Garela—CEO "Team Lulu" East Coast. You're the best!

To Ali, Jade, Jazzie, and Brett—thanks for all your support. Jade's endless desire to help out, Jazzie's makeup moxie, Ali—who could ask for a better friend, and Brett—thanks for keeping us all in check . . . ha, ha.

To Randy Goldberger, for encouraging me to hold my first cooking class on Nantucket.

To Mister Pickles and Sweet Pea, for always putting a smile on my face.

To Bella— you're tough and sweet, all wrapped in one . . . thanks!

To "Team Lulu"—all the wonderful crew of people I have working for me on a continual basis in my catering business. You're all the tops!

The Uziellis—Pinkie and Lucky—you're my girls. Kimm and Al, you never cease to amaze me— thank you!

The Lovett clan—bribery in the form of lipsticks, Barbies, nail polish, and candy. Thank you for letting me bribe—it definitely worked! The kids were terrific.

To Tony Williams—thank you for introducing me to "smart" party. And also for keeping my husband occupied with backgammon while trying to do this book.

To Dan Stern and Eddie Lampert, for suggesting I try Los Angeles on that bleak day of October 27, 1993. "You can always come back," they said.

If you take anything from this book, please may it be that entertaining is fun. Have no fear. Learn some tricks from the trade—and just do it. Enjoy!

X LULU

To Clive Piercy—all Englishmen aren't such a PITA. Thanks for "getting" my "methodical" approach to life. You are a very "clever" man . . .

To Sue Powers Oleary—thank you for helping me strategize . . . boy, did we have some good laughs.

To the Rainwaters, Watkins, Williams, Taylors, Menschels, Mendhels, Schutts, and Rosens—thanks for getting me started.

To DP—"Hey, Buddy!"

The Segel clan— glad you're back in the States. May there be many occasions to "cocktail."

To everyone who came to the photo shoots: Todd Feder; Kendra and Konstantin, Dewey; Stephanie, Georgie, and Maddie Nicks; Jenny "Morty," Billie, and Emmy Morton; Goldie, Spero, Nicholas, Jack, and Caroline; Vein, Christina Odelfelt, a.k.a. Blondie; Megan Bell; Michael Dupont; Coleman McCartan; Tory Vought; Randall Harris; Claudia Benvenuto; Bob Ireland, Ronni Saxon, a.k.a. RTI; Monique Nash; Jeff Raposa; Tina Segel; Deanna Schlesinger; Rick Berge; Tiffany Sacks; Jodi Meyer; Ashley and Ralph Williams; Birchie and Quinnie Kellogg; Alex Killian; Caleigh and Brittany O'Leary; Su Su and Pop Kellogg; Stephanie Landes; Mitchell Peck; Vanessa Coifman; Tessa Benson; Bunky Vroom and Carol and Gordon Gabram.

To Sarah Stately Powers—thank you, thank you, thank you. I would have never made it through the first photo shoot without you. I love you, kid! We used to say working for Mom was "slave labor"; did you think that that day?

To Lee Fowler, for your continued encouragement throughout the years.

Many of those who know me well know that I call everyone "buddy." I even had my friend DP name a cream cheese after me that was called "Hey, Buddy." There are so many people in my life that mean a lot to me each in his or her own unique way. There are way too many of you to list, so to all my buddies out there—you know who you are. Thanks for being a friend!

INDEX